Joys of Computer Networking

The Personal Connection Handbook

Judy Barrett

McGraw-Hill Book Company
New York   St. Louis   San Francisco
Hamburg   Toronto   Mexico

1 2 3 4 5 6 7 8 9   8 7 6 5 4

LIBRARY OF CONGRESS CATALOGING IN PUBLICATION DATA
Barrett, Judy.
Joys of computer networking.
1. Computer networks—Popular works.   2. Data transmission systems—Popular works.
3. Information networks—Popular works.   I. Title.
TK5105.5.B37   1984   384   84-12226
ISBN 0-07-003768-X

A Bard Productions Book
Editing: David J. Morris
Cover Design: Terrence Fehr
Cover Photography: Stan Kearl
Text Design: Mary Ann Noretto
Text Illustrations: Mike Krone
Composition: Typeware, Inc.
Production: The Composing Stick

Contents

Preface

The primary purpose of this book is to help nontechnical people discover some of the entertaining, informative, and useful things that can be done through electronic networking, things that you can do without a shred of technical expertise. Many of the people who are now taking advantage of networking are those who know about or work with computers. That need not be the case. This book has been written to help make your transition into the world of computer networking easy, effective, and rewarding.

Eight years ago I knew nothing about computers. Not only did I know nothing—I was perfectly happy, blissfully secure, and a bit arrogant about my ignorance. After all, what were computers? Big, complicated, expensive adding machines. They were those irritating things that messed up my phone bill and didn't have enough sense to know it. They were the ones who sent me tacky form letters trying to convince me to buy something I didn't want or need, letters they thought I was dumb enough to believe were personal because my name was typed in purple ink. Computers were as foreign as space ships and advanced calculus and about as intimidating.

Well, finally I could avoid it no longer. (That time seems to come to all of us at one point or another.) I went to work for a computer software company. Mine was a purely nontechnical position, but still I could not avoid all the hardware or all the talk of software and interfaces and systems. And I had to admit that it was just a little bit interesting. Here were people doing all sorts of amazing things with little boxes attached to screens, and I had no idea what they were doing. So I broke down and took my first class. It was a simple class in how to use the computer for word processing.

Once I got over being scared to death that I was going to blow up the corporate mainframe computer, it turned out, like so many things, to be fun. It was so nice to be able to type an article once and then make corrections at will without having to worry about hours of retyping. Gradually, I learned more. I learned that those people in the technical department weren't from another planet, that they were really interesting people doing some fascinating things—and even more exciting, I could understand something of what they were doing. My friends in the technical department, Skip and Chip (they have names like that a lot in the technical department), showed me some pretty nifty things I could do with my terminal using a few simple commands. I learned how to make the computer do what I wanted it to do, but I never did understand why it did it. That distinction is an essential thing to remember if you have no plans to become technically sophisticated. **Lots** of people operate computers entirely by rote. They (we) learn the required commands that make the computer do the desired task and then punch those commands in without any notion of why it works—and it works exactly as it would if the reasons were all known.

I am not a programmer, a hacker, a mathematician or a technical whiz by any stretch of the imagination. And I never will be, because that is not where my interests lie. But I have become someone who uses and enjoys computers. It seems clear that computers, unlike beehive hairdos, CB radios and horn-rimmed glasses, are not a passing fad. They are a fact of life that is here to stay.

Relax and enjoy. The following chapters will not transform you into a technical wizard, but they will let you in on some of the secrets those wizards have kept to themselves for too long!

Joys of Computer Networking

Introduction

Try to imagine the computer revolution as an extended range of mountains. From a distance, the peaks look much the same—interesting, but pretty craggy and formidable to most of us. After all, we've heard the stories about mountain climbers who trained for years to scale a single peak. But as we draw closer, we see that all the mountains are not alike. Some are indeed foreign and intimidating; others have gentle slopes, inviting meadows. Computer networking is like one of those meadows. In the technical areas of computing, much expertise is required, hours of training are demanded and mathematical skills are essential, but electronic networking is a special area in the overall scheme, an area easily mastered.

Computer networking lets you enjoy the speed, efficiency and sophistication of all that technology while remaining an easy peak to scale—and the view from the peak is breathtaking. Networking alone can provide you with hours of entertainment, essential business information and personal contacts that can enrich many areas of both your personal and professional life.

Computer networking has been going on for years, but only recently has the general public learned about this exciting and useful method of communication. For the most part, early networks were

1

places to exchange information through computers about computers. Messages left on bulletin boards dealt with technical problems and solutions, and discussion groups talked about the relative merits of one computer as compared with another. Obviously, the one thing all these people had in common was that they had a computer.

Computers are no longer the only thing being discussed on networks. For a while people used their computers to talk about their computers; now they talk about anything and everything under the sun.

The beauty of computer networking is that it does not demand that you acquire technical knowledge in order to take advantage of its wide offerings. While working with personal computers in a business environment may require either programming skills or access to a programmer, that is not true for networking. Anyone who has the necessary equipment can gain information, spend leisure time and share ideas by hooking into electronic networks. This book is written for nontechnical people, people who are new to computers or people who choose to use computers purely by rote. Both novice users and old hands use computer networks in exactly the same ways. Anyone—with or without computing skills, with or without an interest in computers—can use, enjoy and benefit from electronic networks.

The purpose of this book is to let you know about the great wealth of information, services and fun that are available to you through electronic networks. Other books on the market deal with networking as one of the many things you can do in the field of electronic communications. They describe the databases and provide lists of phone numbers, but the personal element is often missing. This book, however, is primarily concerned with how people use their machines to connect with other people. Included in the following chapters are stories about how hundreds of real people use their computers to make contact with each other, to make friends, business associates, sometimes even marriages. Some of these people know all the ins and outs of computing; others know a lot about medicine or publishing or literature. What they have in common is curiosity and a willingness to try a new method of communication. They have a desire to get to know new people and new things and an urge to share something of themselves with other people.

Networking is essentially about sharing—information, facts, expertise, personal experiences, time and energy. Networking is communication in a new way that combines the best of the old ways: when you use your computer to network, you have the speed and directness of a telephone call plus the precision of the written word.

In the following chapters you will learn about the many different kinds of networks. Networks can be invaluable as a tool in your business, whether you are operating a cottage industry out of your home or managing a million dollar stock portfolio. They can broaden your knowledge in any field that interests you, whether for fun or profit. Networks allow you to learn at home at your own pace, to fit your own schedule. Whether you are interested in picking up a course of general interest or want to complete your degree, a network can help meet your needs.

There is not an area in your life that cannot be touched by electronic networks. People are meeting and falling in love through networks. They are making close friends and building relationships that thrive despite distance. They are having fun playing games or reading about new movies. They are planning campaigns, winning elections, debating public policy and communicating with their lawmakers—all through electronic networks.

Despite the advantages of the information age, people find themselves more and more isolated from each other. They work on their own tasks, speak into dictaphones, type into computers or typewriters. Networking offers a definite benefit in that it brings people back in touch with each other. It allows direct communication between distant locations, all from the comfort of your own home or office.

Networking is still in its early stages, but the potential uses are mind-boggling. It is an exciting arena that encompasses possibilities ranging from a Saturday night date—to a new marketing strategy—to world peace. The information that follows will let you decide how you can best benefit from electronic networks. It will give you a feeling for the exciting options that exist for you with your personal computer and modem, and encourage you to join with others who are enjoying the view from the top of the hill.

1

Making Electronic Networking Personal

What Is Computer Networking?

Everyone has some experience with fads. How many of us have dusty CB radios, hula hoops and mood rings tucked away in the attic? Personal computers are undoubtedly a fad. They are the hot topic of cocktail party conversation, the latest status symbol for everyone from six to sixty, the star of stage, screen and TV commercials. The real question is: Can a personal computer really help me enjoy life more, make more money, run my business more efficiently and make me smarter? The real answer is: Yes, especially if you take advantage of its networking capabilities.

A personal computer can be whatever you want it to be. It can be a fun toy you play with for a while and then put into the closet with your CB, or it can become a functioning, enhancing part of your life. A problem many new computer owners face is finding out what to do with the machine besides playing Space Invaders or filing recipes or balancing their checkbooks. These may be handy things to do, but they hardly justify an investment of hundreds, maybe thousands, of dollars.

Computers Are Communication Devices

Electronic networking is one of the answers. Electronic networking can immediately broaden the scope of what your computer can do for you. It can make your small computer with limited capabilities into a large computer with unlimited options. It can transform a small tool into a treasure house of tools for hundreds of uses.

Using only the computer in your home and a few pieces of software, what you can do is limited. Many units come with word processing software, a programming language, maybe a game or two, and a data storage program. That takes care of your checkbook, recipes, and letters to mother, and lets your kids write "Happy Birthday" to be repeated ad infinitum. If you are not a programmer, however, or do not conduct business out of your house, you soon run out of genuinely useful things to do.

With electronic networking, however, your computer is no longer a solitary unit sitting there waiting for a new chicken Kiev recipe. It is a window on the world; it is a link with ideas and people you might otherwise never encounter. Networking lets you keep in touch with people you know and meet hundreds of people you didn't know before.

The personal computer and electronic networking have the potential of changing the way people communicate just as dramatically as the telephone and television did. Telephone and television have made news instantaneous. The world continues to shrink because of the immediate ways that people can link up with each other electronically. Networking is another way that electronics can make communication easier and more timely.

Once you begin to think of your computer as a communications device, the idea becomes simpler and easier to imagine. Whatever your field of interest, there are other people in the world who share that interest. The problem in the past has been to locate those people. Now electronic networking simplifies that problem by helping you find those people without ever having to leave home. And your interest does not have to lie with computers—they are only the tool, the medium through which your knowledge and the knowledge of other people is communicated.

When electronic networking began, it was mostly concerned with computers. A mystique grew up that said you had to be a computer expert and talk about such things as baud rate to be able to use networking. Obviously the one thing that networkers have in common is that they all own and use computers. That is also true of people who use the telephone, yet we do not feel constrained to talk about long distance rates when we make a phone call.

The diversity possible with networking is just beginning to be tapped. As more and more nontechnical people buy computers and begin talking to each other, the fields of discussion will expand rapidly. Already there are ongoing on-line discussions about art, medicine, hang gliding and hundreds of other noncomputer topics.

The creation of large information utilities like CompuServe and The Source has also made electronic networking simple and economical. A man in Texas and his close friend in New Hampshire have found that they can keep in touch through CompuServe for less money than it takes to make long-distance phone calls. They simply dial a local number at a prearranged time and conduct their conversation through their home computers. The cost of connect time with CompuServe is less than the cost of a phone call would be, and, if they wish, they can also have a permanent record of the conversation. During the evenings and on weekends, when they would normally call to chat anyway, they can talk for an hour on CompuServe for only $6. They can also leave messages for each other on the service, rather than calling again and again only to find the other not at home or already on the phone. These same two men are now contemplating setting up a business together— with one partner in New Hampshire, the other in Texas. They will use electronic networking to ensure that the business operates smoothly and that information is passed quickly between the manufacturing plant in New Hampshire and the administrative office in Texas.

One of the best things about networking is that it can be arranged to fit your own needs. Networking can be worldwide or it can be simply between you and one other person. It can involve all the members of a specific group, like a local political unit, or it can extend to everyone who owns a personal computer. It can be done in the middle of the night on top of a mountain in West Virginia or during prime time in the comfort of your home or in a phone

booth at the corner of Hollywood and Vine. The beauty of electronic networking is that it is both flexible and fast. It is not
something that you must do during regular business hours or from
a particular location. You can decide when and where you are ready
to communicate.

Now that fear of computers is fading, people want to know more
about them. What can you do besides play games on them? How
can the personal computer streamline communications and make
your life more like you want it to be? Can the personal computer
help you meet new people, find new information, be more creative?
The answers to all these questions lie in the use of personal computers for electronic networking.

Networking is communication—people talking to people. Like
many phrases that become popular, "electronic networking" has
taken on a mysterious sound. You think it must be complicated,
require technical knowledge, or, at the very least, involve large
amounts of money. These are simply misconceptions. When you
go to a bar and strike up a conversation with another person, you
need no complicated skills or subtle methods. You simply sit down
and begin to chat. What begins as inane chatter can sometimes
develop into a genuine friendship. The same is true of electronic
networking. You don't have to know how a computer works to talk
with people on a computer, any more than you have to know how
a telephone works to talk with people on the phone.

Don't let the jargon complicate things. You could say "I'm going
to instigate telecommunications with my Aunt Fanny," or you could
say "I'm calling Aunt Fanny on the phone." In either case, you're
doing the same thing. Similarly, you can say "I'm going to interface electronically with a utility network and exchange data with
fellow instrumentalists," or you could say, "I'm going to call up
some people on the computer and talk about music." It's two ways
of saying the same thing.

Computer wizards can network with their computers. Computer
novices can network with their computers just as well. You don't
have to know how it works, you don't have to write a program,
you don't have to speak the language. You just have to know a few
tricks to get going. You have to know how to punch the phone buttons to call up Aunt Fanny and you have to know which keyboard
buttons to push to call up fellow musicians. There's no mystery,

no arcane knowledge required, just a little simple instruction, and a whole new world of useful conversation is opened up to you. Everyone has seen models of the universe. Planets revolve around suns. Smaller suns and moons and planets follow their orbits on their paths through the heavens. Distant stars shine with varying degrees of brightness. At first glance, all the movement looks random and complex, but in fact laws govern the movement and keep things from crashing into each other. Oh, occasionally one of the stars burns itself out or a new star is born—but for the most part, there is order in the universe.

The world of electronic networking is comparable to that model. There are giant mainframes out there and minis and micros, dumb terminals float around and bulletin boards spring up and disappear. And even if you can't understand the complexities of the system, you can still be a part of it. Think of your own computer or word processor or terminal as a magic carpet that can transport you to any place in the universe. *No one* expects you to know how magic carpets work!

Hopping on your magic carpet is the easiest, most comfortable and most convenient way to find and share information. You can drop in on a discussion of environmental concerns, for instance, to see if it interests you. If the ongoing discussion is right up your alley, you can jump in and become a part of the group. If the topic is not really what you're looking for, you're free to bow out. And it is perfectly acceptable to hop on that carpet and fly whenever you're ready.

Joining an electronic network does not involve a commitment to continue participation in the group. The rules of etiquette are very relaxed. Just about all anyone expects is that you say goodbye before you leave.

Why Network?

People network for a variety of reasons, but the most common are for information and for fun. Just as some people talk on the phone to give or receive information or simply to keep in touch with friends, people talk on the computer for the same reasons. Electronic networking allows you to get and give information, and it allows you to meet new people and keep in touch with old friends.

Everything that can be said for networking on a small or local scale can also be said about computer/electronic networking— except that the scale becomes global. With computer networking, you can communicate with people half a continent or half a world away. You can get information from experts that you would otherwise never have the opportunity to meet. Even in your own city there are people who have information you want, but in many cases you don't know about them. Through computer networking, you can identify and contact these people quickly and easily.

What Is Needed to Network?

Most people are surprised that networking can be done with a minimal investment. Of course, the sophistication of your system is completely up to you, but it needs to be stressed that you don't have to spend a lot of money, have fancy hardware and software or be a computer whiz to begin networking—now. You can enjoy the process, meet people and participate fully in this new form of communication with modest equipment. Chapter 2 tells in detail what sort of equipment you may need in order to begin electronic networking, but what follows will give you a brief summary of some of the choices.

THE ESSENTIALS
The Communicator

The first thing you need is a device to send your words and receive other people's words: a computer, a terminal or a word processor. This machine can be a simple keyboard that plugs into your TV or a sophisticated piece of hardware that does everything but tap dance. Prices for the basic unit range from less than $100 to more than $10,000. Any computer can be made to communicate regardless of price or brand name.

The Connector

To connect your terminal or word processor or computer to the outside world, you need a modem. Modems can be inexpensive little cradles to fit your telephone receiver into, or they can be direct connectors to the phone lines that can dial for you and answer the phone when you're away. Prices of the units go up as they begin to do more things for you.

The Organizer

In order for information to be sent electronically from one place to another, it must be broken down and transmitted over phone lines. A serial card organizes the information so that it can be sent and understood by the communicating machines. Many computers come with serial cards built in, others have to have them added, but to communicate you must have one.

The Interpreter

When computers communicate with each other they don't speak English, they beep. To understand those beeps, you need communications software. This is a computer program that changes beeps into the words they began as and changes the words into beeps to be sent out.

These four items, along with a telephone, are all you need to begin electronic networking. You can buy everything listed above for as little as $300.

While you may want to begin electronic networking with minimum expense, there are a lot of additional items that you can add to your system either later or right away. These options, also called peripherals, add power and flexibility to your system. You may want to have a printer so that you can make a copy of your conversations for future reference. You may also want disk drives, other kinds of software or a color monitor. The list is long and the options are explained more fully in Chapter 2. Keep in mind, however, that they are *options*. You can have the fun and benefits of computer networking with only the bare necessities.

Ways of Networking

There are several different ways that electronic networking can take place. Depending on your equipment and goals, you may choose some or all of the following.

Messages in a Mailbox

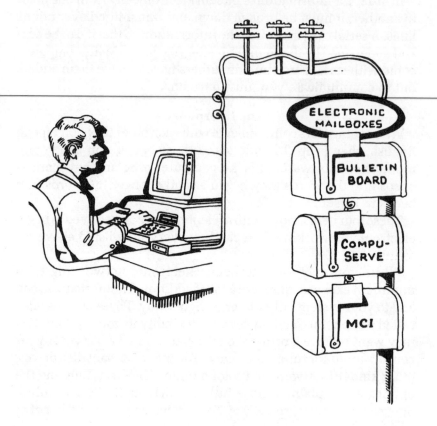

One of the most commonly used networking methods is called electronic mail. Electronic mail is a message sent from one person to another through some sort of computer channel. These mail services can be in a small area—in your office or town—or they can be worldwide. Electronic mail is available through bulletin boards, utilities, and through some telephone services, like MCI. Don't worry if some of these terms sound like the names of strange beasts; they will all be explained.

The point to understand now about electronic mail is that it is a way to send a message to another person quickly and efficiently. The other person does not have to be at home or at the computer. You send your message and when the person reads that message, he or she can send a reply back to you.

Many local bulletin boards provide mailboxes for their users. The large utilities have mailboxes. In either case, your correspondent simply addresses a message to you, and the message is there when you sign onto the system. In most cases when you sign on there is a note that says you have mail and asks if you want to read it immediately.

Electronic mail privacy depends on the system you are using. There is some concern about privacy, but for the most part your communications are visible only to yourself, the system operator and the addressee. You would probably not want to send highly sensitive, secret information over the line, but few of us send that sort of information anyway.

Postings on a Bulletin Board

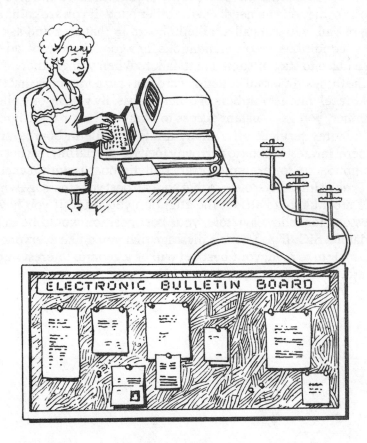

On the other hand, if you want to meet someone new or find new sources of information, a local bulletin board is perhaps your best bet. Bulletin boards (or hobby boards, as they are sometimes called) operate all over the U.S. People who are interested in electronic communication set up these boards and allow the public to access them. Almost all are free within your own city; you can call boards in other cities for the cost of a long-distance phone call. Many who use boards frequently subscribe to discount long-distance services in order to lower their phone bills.

When you call up a bulletin board, one of your options is to post a message. Say, for example, that you are looking for a kennel that specializes in training German shepherds. You can post a notice to that effect on the bulletin board, and anyone on the board knowing of such a kennel will post a reply to your message and give you the information you need. On the other hand, if you are going skiing in Vail, you can call a bulletin board in that area and ask for snow conditions, recommendations for a good restaurant, advice on a place to stay or someone to talk to when you get there. One of the things almost all bulletin boards have in common is that they list the telephone numbers of other boards. By getting one phone number, you gain instant access to boards all over the country.

Videotex services offer many kinds of bulletin boards, from general interest boards to narrowly focused special interest boards. CompuServe, for example, offers bulletin boards within each of its Special Interest Groups so that you can post your message where it is most likely to attract the attention you want. If you have a message for fellow aviators, your best position would be in the Aviator's SIG. If you have a message that you'd like everyone on the system to read, your best bet will be a general interest public board.

Keyboard Chatting

The Source and CompuServe are huge computer installations that allow you to make contact with people you would not ordinarily meet on a local bulletin board. Both charge for their services, but cost depends on the time of day and type of services you want. Once you sign up with one of these utilities, the question is not what you can do, but what you want to do. Both services offer a growing range of options. One of the benefits of the large services over local boards is that conversations can take place in "real time."

That means that you can talk directly to other people rather than leaving a message and waiting for a reply. If you say, "I'm interested in belly dancing" on a bulletin board, you may have to call back hours or days later to see if anyone else shares your interest. If you make the same statement on The Source or CompuServe, you can get an immediate response: "I love belly dancing too and have almost worn out my finger cymbals," or "You must be in the wrong place; this is the special interest group for Jesuit Brothers." Both The Source and CompuServe offer many options for direct communication, ranging from simple chatting on the CB simulator to detailed discussions of technical information to conversations on professional interests. Both offer chat or conference modes in a variety of subject areas as well as other kinds of communication.

Messages Stored with a Modem

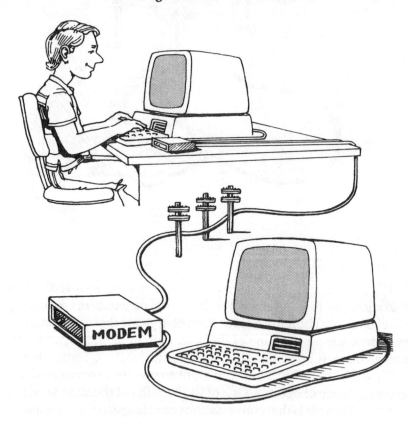

If you expect to have many messages and are not always stand-ing by waiting for a call, or if you don't want to have to dial up a utility or bulletin board to get your mail, you may want to invest in a modem that will answer your phone and store messages that can be transferred later to your computer's memory. If you choose this option, your phone will need to be plugged into the modem at all times, so you will probably want to get a separate telephone line for the computer. The advantage of this choice is that your messages will always be waiting for you to pick them up at your convenience.

Modems that automatically answer calls and store messages are obviously more expensive than those that simply connect your ter-minal to the phone lines. Still, if you are involved in information gathering or have a very active computer social life, you may decide that this is the way to go.

Networking at Work

Many businesses have what are called Local Area Networks (LANs). This means that all the computers in the company—whether in a single location or spread across the country—are connected to each other. Although there are many uses for LANs, one of the most frequently used options is communications. People can leave mail for you on the LAN and you can check your messages whenever it is convenient. You need not be in your office when the message is sent—the LAN will hold it for you. LANs also allow direct communication back and forth between offices—a sort of conferencing that allows decisions to be made quickly and easily.

Although LANs are primarily business systems, they are also used for networking. People communicate and meet each other through the networks; like the office coffeepot, LANs serve to bring employees into closer communication. Many colleges and universities utilize LANs to tie the various departments and disciplines together more closely.

Networks can also be invaluable business tools to people who work at home or who work in a company that doesn't have a local area network. Hundreds of business services are available on-line; in addition, networks give you the opportunity to talk with people in your field, make important business connections and advertise your services or products for minimal costs.

Whatever business communications needs you have, you can find a network that will serve those needs. Not only do the networks help your career, they will also help you take care of your personal business and financial needs by keeping you up-to-date on trends, giving you access to sophisticated computation programs and even allowing you to bank by computer.

Keyboard to Mailpouch

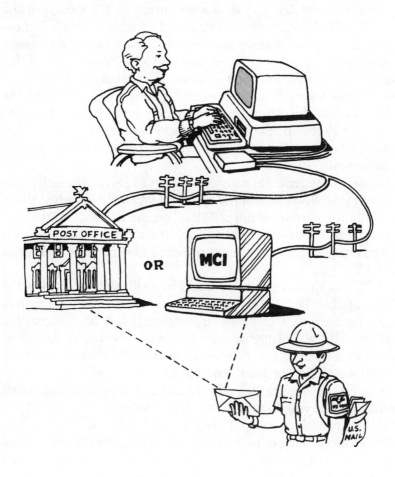

One fast-growing method of electronic networking involves a combination of electronic and more conventional types of communication. Many people realize that sending mail electronically is both quicker and more efficient than dictating and typing letters. Getting those messages to the proper place, however, is not always simple. Some of the people you want to address do not have electronic mailboxes or even computers. In that case, you can have the advantages of both electronic and conventional mail.

The U.S. Post Office has an electronic mail service called E-COM. Designed primarily for large businesses or frequent mailers, this system requires that you send a minimum of 200 messages at a time. The Post Office also has stringent requirements about how your system operates and sends mail. Because of the requirements, few hobby networkers will be using E-COM directly, but if you are marketing a product and wish to send a lot of electronic mail, the system is very fast and economical. For little more than the price of a first class stamp, you can send your messages in record time. The Post Office will either send your messages to another computer or turn them into written words and deliver them by regular mail.

If you do not generate enough mail to use E-COM directly, you can still take advantage of the system if you are a member of one of the national information utilities. You can use E-COM through The Source, CompuServe or Delphi. It costs more than the Post Office charges, but you are not required to send large quantities of mail.

MCI has a similar service which is more likely to be used by the general public because it does not require many pieces of mail to be sent at once, and the charge is less than that of the information utilities. MCI will also guarantee that if your correspondent does not have a receiving computer the mail will be hand-delivered within four hours of your sending it.

In addition to quick delivery, MCI also has laser printers that can reproduce your logo, trademark or whatever other design you want imprinted on your letters.

There are a number of services which convert electronic mail to printed material and deliver it quickly. Western Union, Telenet and Tymnet are among the businesses which offer this service. If you are a networker operating a small business, the options are worth checking into because of their ease of use, economy and speed.

Networking Options

Other networks fall somewhere between the local bulletin boards and the giant utilities. These are pay networks set up for special purposes. Some of them are politically oriented, others are concerned with specific professions and still others provide information for a price. Once you begin electronic networking, you will find the options growing. My experience has been that the people who enjoy electronic networking are more than happy to share their information. Because they think it is all a great idea, they want everyone else to share their enthusiasm and are eager to tell you what other choices are out there. For example, if you want to know who is using the same kind of computer you are using, check with your bulletin board for a users' group. If you are having some problems or want to ask a fellow IBM user about a particular type of software, all you have to do is connect electronically with a member of the group and a dialogue is set in motion.

The subject matter of networks is almost limitless. Anything that people are interested in is a suitable topic for a network—and there is probably a network already going on that topic somewhere.

When you tap into one of the nationwide utilities like CompuServe or The Source, your range of networking capabilities is immediately multiplied a thousandfold. Within the Services for Professionals Area in CompuServe, for example, there are forums for people in aviation, fire protection, communications, environmental concerns, law, medicine, dentistry, veterinary medicine, music and on and on. These groups let you find out what other professionals in your field are doing, what the newest developments are, what innovative techniques are being tried and what job opportunities are available. They also allow you to share your experiences and expertise.

But networking is not limited to professional concerns. Networking can be any kind of personal information sharing. You can meet people who share your hobbies, enjoy playing the same games you enjoy, have equipment you want to buy or just want to make friends.

There are CB groups for casual chatting which can be used just like CB radios. There are personal columns for people who are looking for new friends—both casual and intimate. There are electronic flea markets that allow you to buy what you need. There are opportunities for making your creative abilities known to others. The list is almost endless and all of these possibilities fall under the umbrella of networking—specifically, electronic networking.

Electronic networking will never take the place of face-to-face relationships. It will not solve all your problems, but it can greatly enrich your life and provide opportunities that would not otherwise exist. And, of course, electronic networking can, and often does, lead to more personal kinds of relationships. People who initially meet through electronic networking are free to establish contact through phone calls or meetings. When you go to a meeting of the local Audubon Society, you will meet people you'd like to see again or talk with or lunch with; similarly you will meet people through electronic networking that you'd like to get to know better. Electronic networking simply gives you more options, more information more quickly and a broader geographical range in which to find new people.

Almost every story in this book is a result of electronic networking. When I first began hearing about electronic networks, I thought, "Oh, great, another way for techies to debate the merits of MS-DOS vs CP/M."

I quickly burned out on techie-talk. The worst thing about listening to technical talk, aside from understanding little of it, is that it is so intimidating. So I did not leap into electronic networking without some trepidation. Although I wasn't a total novice with computers, I was—and am—far from being a technical expert. In fact, on my maiden voyage into electronic networking, I insisted that a technically sophisticated friend be there to hold my hand and tell me what to do.

We began by looking at local bulletin boards, and as it turned out, all I really needed my expert for was to tell me the first phone number.

The most exciting thing about bulletin boards (described in more detail in Chapter 3) is that they are incredibly simple to use. The first one we called began by asking my name. Good, I could do that. It then asked if I had ever used that board before or if I was new. I told it "New," and the board proceeded to tell me everything I needed to know in plain English—really, plain English. (There are some software packages that talk about English-like commands and English-based language, but end up saying things like GOTO, DBMS, and ROR. Although they are relatively simple to learn, they are not "plain English.") The bulletin board simply said: Here's what you can do, here's how to do it, and if you get lost or confused, type "?" and you'll get some help. That's plain English!

Pretty soon I was dialing up numbers all by myself. Once or twice a board asked me a question I either didn't understand or didn't know the answer to: "How many nulls?" or "What is your line length?" In those cases, I just made something up and asked my expert later. One board asked me if I needed line feed. At that time I was working on a borrowed terminal and had no idea whether I needed line feed—or, for that matter, what line feed was. So I took a chance and said no. Well, when the words began to appear one on top of another, on a single line, I guessed that maybe I did need line feed after all. So I simply typed "help" and went back and corrected my error. Several boards went so far as to assure me that I could not blow up the whole system. I appreciated that.

After getting my feet wet and eavesdropping on other people's messages, I began to leave messages of my own. Every step of the way the board held my hand and told me what my choices were. That was good enough, but when messages began coming back to me, I became a true believer.

Having done research, I know how many days, weeks, even months can be eaten up just trying to find out who knows what I need to know. Using electronic networks, I found a whole group of people in a few hours. It really worked, and it worked without having to learn jargon or secret codes. It worked for me, and although I was a bit deflated, I was also delighted to learn that it worked for my 10- and 13-year-old daughters just as well.

After more experimenting, I became more experienced and knowledgeable. There are plenty of opportunities and simple ways to learn. The best part of networking is that you can go at your own pace, learn as little—or as much—as you want to learn, and still enjoy the experience. More than an event, it is a process. It is a way to accomplish your goals while learning.

Electronic networking, like almost any other form of communication, requires little more than courage to get started—and once you've started, it's such fun you don't want to stop.

2

Hardware, Software—
Choices, Choices, and
More Choices

What Do I Need to Network?

Unless you want to be a programming whiz, the hardest thing about computers is shopping for and buying them. If you're lucky, you've done that and lived to tell about it and are now ready to enjoy the fruits of your labor. If you don't already have your machinery, here's a little information about what you need (and what you can have even if you don't need it) for electronic networking.

There are several problems with buying computer software and hardware. Most of them, however, are merely annoying and can be overcome with patience and a bit of humor. The computer novice who embarks on a trip to the computer store faces two problems. The first is vocabulary. Computer salespeople, programmers, developers and manufacturers have decided that to set themselves apart from the rest of us mere mortals, they should speak a foreign language. And they do. Fluently. We have two choices here as I see it. Either we can capitulate and learn their words, or we can insist on plain English. I believe strongly that the power of right and justice are squarely behind the second option.

Computer Talk

Almost everything that the average person needs to say about computers can be said in ordinary English. There are, however, a few terms that you simply can't avoid. Some of these things just didn't exist until computers came along and made them up. A brief vocabulary lesson, therefore, is in order. These are a few of the most often used words. Others are explained as we go along and still others are defined in the back of the book.

Users—You and I are users. Sad as it may seem with its implications of illegal substances, addiction and all that, *user* is the word widely accepted to describe a person who uses computers. Programmers program, systems analysts analyze, data processors process and users use. The meaning is that we take advantage of all the technology without knowing its ins and outs. Actually, it is a lot more fun to be a user than most of those other things.

RAM—This is really popular with salespeople. They race up to you when you walk in the door and say "How much RAM do you need?" *RAM* stands for Random Access Memory. What that refers to is how much stuff your computer can store at one time. If you are using a very sophisticated and powerful software package, you may need large amounts of memory. Generally, however, 64K RAM will take care of most things nicely and is a standard capacity for personal machines. For networking you actually need no RAM at all.

K—*K* stands for a kilobyte or a thousand bytes. You don't really need to know all this, but they'll be talking about it so it might not hurt to know. Bytes are the symbols that make up the characters (letters, numbers, punctuation marks, etc.) that you type into your machine. The machine translates each character into eight symbols or bits. Eight bits make a byte. (A nibble, on the other hand, is half a byte or usually four bits.) But a byte is not exactly a character, because there have to be spaces and such, so nothing really comes out even. The point is that bits and bytes are like pints and quarts and are ways that computers measure storage space and length of material. When they say "64K," they are talking about 64,000 bytes of data that can be stored at one time in the computer's memory.

Peripherals—These are the additional things you can buy to go with your computer. Modems, printers, monitors and other accessories are all peripherals if they don't come already built into your computer.

The second major problem in buying hardware and software is that there are so many choices. When you begin looking into electronic networking equipment, you soon realize that there are literally hundreds of items from which to choose.

Hardware is the machine itself. Personal computers, desk-top computers, briefcase computers, pocket computers, terminals, word processors, modems—all the things that you can see and touch—are pieces of hardware. *Software* packages are programs that make the hardware do what you want it to do. To use a time-honored analogy that is tossed around in the trade, hardware is the record player, the speaker, the knobs and switches; software is the music that plays on the machinery.

Software comes stored on floppy disks, cartridges and in another form called *firmware.* Firmware—obviously somewhere between hard and soft—is programs that are permanently stored in your computer. You can't take them out or change them, and in most cases you can't even tell they are there except that they make the computer do things it would not otherwise do. Some computers come with certain functions already in place—word processing, for example. You don't have to buy a word-processing package or insert a word-processing disk; it is already there in the firmware. Other computers come without firmware and you add all the programs, or directions, to the machine in the form of software.

To network, you need both hardware and software. You need a computer, communicating word processor or terminal, a modem and a communications card. Because most people are opting for computers, I will concentrate on them. If you decide to buy a word processor or terminal, you don't have to worry about peripherals, communications cards, and, in the case of terminals, software.

Kinds of Hardware

There are three basic types of computers: mainframes, minis and micros. Mainframe computers are those large, powerful machines that you first saw in pictures years ago. Although mainframes no longer run on vacuum tubes and therefore do not have to be kept in frozen airtight rooms, they are still highly sensitive.

You have to know how to talk to them; you have to keep them cool; and you have to pay a lot of money for them. Mainframe computers are incredibly powerful. They can transmit data at high speed, perform complex calculations before you can blink an eye and do all sorts of complicated things. When you are networking through one of the information utilities, you are probably using mainframe computers. They are wonderful inventions, but you'll probably never have one in your home.

Minicomputers are smaller and less powerful than mainframes, but they are still relatively large machines with a great deal of flexibility and computational ability. Many people can use the same minicomputer at the same time, just as they do with mainframes. Corporations often use minicomputers for all their business activities.

Microcomputers are our main interest here. All personal or home computers are micros. The microcomputer is a relative newcomer to the field, and consequently the market is bursting with competitive models and the attendant confusion. No one really knows all that the microcomputer is capable of doing. New possibilities are being explored constantly. Right now, microcomputers are best known for their personal qualities. Used by only one person at a time, a micro allows you to do all your work or pleasure activities on a computer without having to share your information with anyone else. Your files are kept on a disk or tape or in the memory of your machine, and no one has access to those files unless you agree. Micros have also made it feasible for individuals to own computers. Until the micro was developed, all computers were so expensive that only businesses or the very rich could justify the expense. It's the combination of price and personal control that makes microcomputers so attractive.

Microcomputers come in a wide variety of styles and sizes. The first micros were relatively large machines that you had to put down where you wanted them to stay. Many micros are still large and heavy. If you plan to network in a different town each day, you would do well to get a small machine, but if you plan to do all your networking at the desk in your den, size is of little consequence. Before you begin shopping, however, you should be aware that there are many different sizes from which to choose. Desk-top models are the most common and are what you see when you go to a business establishment that uses personal computers. Then there are portable models of various sizes. Some look like desk-top models with a handle on one side; others are compact and lightweight. Next come briefcase models that fit into a briefcase and are easily carried anywhere.

Hardware Homework

Before you ever step into a computer store, you should have some idea of what you want the machine to do. That is not to say that you need to know what you are going to buy or even that you'll end up with what you had in mind in the first place. But, you need to know what your principal uses for the machine will be. Sadly, there aren't yet any truly all-purpose personal computers on the market. The industry is still too new for much standardization to have occurred, so what has happened is that one system concentrates on games, another on word processing, another on programming, still another on educational packages, and many others on business uses.

When you begin to think about buying a computer, consider which members of your family are apt to use it and what they will be using it for. Then when the salesperson asks questions, you'll have some answers ready. With all the capabilities of personal computers, it seems silly to buy a one-function machine, so look for as much flexibility as possible. As far as networking goes, all home computers are made to communicate, with appropriate modifications or additions. Some are now being made with built-in communications packages, others with built-in modems, and still others with built-in communications cards, but even if yours does not have these items included, they can be added.

There are a lot of choices to make when you are purchasing a computer. You can buy complete systems—ready to communicate, print, store files, do any number of things—or you can buy your system a piece at a time. The computer, or central processing unit (CPU), is the part that computes, holds information in its memory and works for you. Generally, the working part of your computer is in the keyboard. If you have a personal computer keyboard, you have a computer. Of course, you will need some way to see what you are doing, so you will need a cathode ray tube (CRT). The CRT can be a television set you already own—either black-and-white or color—or it can be a computer monitor that is sold with your unit. Some computer manufacturers build modular computers designed for the person who wants to begin small and add components as the need and cash arise. Other companies build only complete units, with keyboard, monitor, disk drives and software all built in.

Hardware Options

There is a lot of talk in the computer industry about "user friendliness." This refers to the ease with which a person can begin using the machine. User friendliness is a claim made by a lot of computer manufacturers, and there is certainly a wide range of friendliness in the machines. To the novice who wants to use a machine for networking of information, ideas and entertainment, the friendlier the better. Many hours, for example, have been put into the Apple Macintosh to make it simple to use. The long hours of development have resulted in a product that does all sorts of complicated things without the user's ever having to know why. The Epson QX10 is also a very friendly machine. It has clearly labeled buttons to start your modem working, dial up the number you're calling and perform a multitude of other tasks.

Radio Shack TRS-80 machines are easy to use because all their software is designed specifically for their machines. They are also a company with a history of consumer marketing—something that many high-tech companies are finding a new experience—and that has helped them design computers that the average consumer can use.

User friendliness is extremely important to the beginning networker, and it continues to be important as you grow more accustomed to communicating electronically. There is no good reason for a machine to be hard to use. Still, friendliness is not the only criterion you need to keep in mind when you're shopping. Unless the machine does what you want it to do, it is useless and frustrating. A friendly machine that can't help balance your budget when you really want to balance your budget is not the machine for you. When thinking about what you want the machine to do, let your imagination roam. First, think of all the things you'd do right now if you had a computer, then try to imagine uses you or members of your family might have in the future. For most of us, the purchase of a computer is a major investment—an investment we'd like to last for a while. So if you have kids, think of ways they might need to use a computer. If you are considering opening a part-time business, think of things you'd need a computer to do for that project. If you have a hobby to keep track of, consider a computer in that area of your life. While you are in the planning and imagining stage, you can have anything you want. Once you begin looking around, you may not find everything you want in one machine at the price you want to pay, but you'll never know until you decide what you want.

Another good idea is to do a little reading before you venture out to look at computers. There are several books and many magazine articles written specifically to help you choose a personal computer. You can be fairly sure that in the first store you visit a salesperson will assure you that their computer is the perfect one. The more information you have before you go shopping, the easier it will be to select a system you'll be happy with.

On the other hand, most of the home computers on the market are really pretty good. The competition is just too stiff for a "dog" to stay on the market long. The companies that make personal computers are anxious to get your business and are working hard to make their products attractive and effective. Odds are that if you're buying a computer for personal use rather than for sophisticated programming or complicated business problems, you'll be happy with any number of machines. You really don't need to feel compelled to look at every product on the market, do a thorough market study or tear out your hair comparing technical specifications. If you find one you like that does what you want and is in your price range, buy it, even if it's the first one you look at. The real fun comes after you get it home and start playing with it. There's no reason to prolong the agony.

Dealing with Dealers

I have no intention of recommending a machine for you to buy. What you want and need are very personal; it's better to look around and talk with as many people as you want before making a decision...which brings us back to that first step into the "hardware store." Although there is a lot of emphasis on user friendliness, computer salespeople are (and I realize this is an unfair generalization) some of the most intimidating people in the world. Although I got over my fear of computers years ago, I'm still a little shaken by computer dealers. They can always ask you a question you can't answer, and they consistently talk as though they have the final word on technical matters. As soon as you walk into the store they begin asking questions in that foreign language. The only advice I can give in dealing with computer salespeople is to try not to be intimidated. Don't allow them to make you feel stupid. Feel free to insist that they explain what they are talking about. After all, they want your business, and it is their responsibility to make their product attractive to you.

One good thing to remember is that there isn't a final word on microcomputers and won't be for several years to come. Whatever was the last word last night is old hat this morning simply because things are changing so fast. (A computer salesperson told me that— proof of the unfairness of generalities.)

Another thing to remember is that even if a salesperson thinks you should be a programmer to own a machine, that is simply not true. I went into a computer shop not long ago to get a new cable. The technician began asking questions about the internal operations of the machine, and of course, I didn't know the answers. I told him I just knew it didn't work and thought a new cable would fix it. "Well," he said, "I can see that you really don't want to know how to use a computer."

He was absolutely wrong, and I did my best to educate him. I know how to use the computer. I don't know how to fix it. I know how to use the washing machine, and I don't know how to fix it either—but the washer repairman never looks down his nose at me for my abysmal ignorance. Most of the people selling computers are young, enthusiastic and completely sold on the technical wonders of the machine. That's great. I'm glad they like their products, and I'll be gladder still when they relax a little and don't demand quite so much of their customers. In the meantime, the best we can do is keep looking and keep talking and not get intimidated completely out of the mood to join the electronic age.

Although the price of personal computers has fallen rapidly and may continue to fall, computers are still not cheap (as most people understand "cheap"). About $300 is the least you can spend for a complete networking setup. And the sky's the limit on the other end of the scale, with a lot of variety in between. Again, how much you spend is determined by what you want to do. There's no point in spending $3,000 or more on an IBM PC, just because it has a famous name, if all you want to do is network. If, however, you want to take advantage of the enormous amount of software available and the power of the machine, then the IBM might be your most sensible purchase.

Among the least expensive computers on the market are the Commodore and Atari models. If you buy one of these computers and attach it to your television, you can put a very economical system into action quickly. Both these vendors began in the videogame business several years ago and are branching out to include computers in their lines. They have experience in dealing with the public and in making their machines easy to use. They have also made sure that their systems are expandable by making modems, printers and software for a variety of uses.

Another toy and game manufacturer, Coleco, introduced one of the most looked-forward-to products of 1983, the Adam. Adam is a personal computer system that includes a keyboard, monitor, disk drives and a printer for less than $1,000.

Many networkers, and others, are very enthusiastic about briefcase-type computers. The Radio Shack TRS-100, named Product of the Year in 1983 by *InfoWorld Magazine,* is beautifully suited for networking. The little machine (weighing in at four pounds) is battery powered, making it ideal for networking anyplace at any time. It comes equipped with a built-in communications package, a modem and some free time on CompuServe. It is small, compact, truly portable and a genuine computer. The firmware consists of five programs: text editor, communications, address book, appointment scheduling and a BASIC interpreter to allow you to write your own programs. Because of the built-in communications package, data can be gathered, stored on another computer, transferred to a tape cassette, printed on a printer or sent to your neighbor down the street who has his own computer and modem. The Model 100 is priced at around $800.

Once you have your machine, you need a communications card or serial port to allow your computer to translate the beeps that come through the phone line back into letters you can read and understand. When you are communicating through phone lines, the signals have to march one after another in a straight line—serially. When you communicate to a printer, you communicate in a parallel manner—eight little signals side by side. That's why you need something to tell your machine, "OK, line them up." More and more computers come with serial interfaces already built in, but not all do. When you are buying equipment, be sure to ask.

Word Processors

People who earn their living as writers, secretaries or in other word-related occupations may want to invest in a communicating word processor rather than a computer. If you plan to do nothing with the machine but process words and network, this may be the best choice. Although computers allow for very good word-processing packages, a dedicated word processor can do more sophisticated things for a professional word worker. Just be sure that when you select your machine, it is a *communicating* word processor. Not all of them are.

Terminals

The other choice is to buy a "dumb terminal": a machine that can't do anything by itself. If you have a computer, you can put in your software and do all sorts of things with your unit, including communicating. When you are communicating, though, your computer pretends that it is a terminal. A dumb terminal, however, can work only when connected with another machine. Many corporations use terminals hooked into a corporate mainframe. This system works well because everyone in the company shares the same mainframe, software and information. A terminal can work for networking, too, because when you call up a bulletin board or CompuServe or any other network, you are using someone else's computer. That's the reason that your computer has to pretend it is only a terminal. While you are on-line, you are an extension of another system and your computer is comparable to a television set. If the stations did not transmit, your TV would do nothing—no pictures, no sound, no information. When you are networking, you are relying on the host computer to provide you with words, pictures and information.

Terminals can be either CRTs or printers with keyboards. The Texas Instruments Silent 700 is a communicating terminal/printer with a built-in acoustic modem and everything you need to network. The only thing you have to do is plug it in and start dialing. Computers are obviously a lot more flexible and can do many more things than terminals can. On the other hand, terminals don't offer the myriad opportunities for frustration and confusion that computers do either. If you prefer a terminal, or if you already have one, by all means use it. It is excellent for networking. The only major drawback with a CRT-type terminal is that once the information has passed across your screen, it's gone. If your terminal prints, you do have a record of your conversation.

Videotex terminals are an exception to standard dumb terminals. Designed specifically for data communications, machines like the Quik-Link from Quazon provide features for networking that dumb terminals do not, and they are economical. The Quik-Link, for example, is priced at $249 and comes with more than $200 worth of registration fees and/or trial-use time in the most popular national information services. It includes some message storage space, and since it is not a computer, there are fewer commands and rules to learn in order to begin operating it.

Software Options

If you have a computer, you also need a software or firmware package that is designed for communication. As mentioned, some machines come with built-in firmware for that purpose. Most do not. The communications software allows your computer to act as a terminal and controls how your modem works. It can also allow you to download files, save communications on a disk and contribute files of your own to someone else's system. There are numerous software packages available. Your first consideration is that the software run on your machine. The biggest nuisance of computer technology right now is that there are so many systems, each system requiring different software. So you must be sure that the software you are considering will work with your hardware.

Communications software offers many variations. Some only serve to turn your computer into a dumb terminal. These packages are often called things like "Dumb Term" and "Terminal Emulator." You will be able to communicate with that kind of package, but you will not be able to save any of the information you receive unless you also have a printer hooked up to your system. In order to save data you've gotten on a network for further manipulation with your own computer, your software must provide a download option. Downloading means that you save something you find on-line in your computer's memory or on a disk or cassette once the on-line session is over. You may decide to keep conversations with a new friend, data gathered about a business venture or a program for balancing your checkbook. To do that, your software must have a download option. This option is also referred to as "file transfer capability."

Uploading is another form of file transfer. Just as you download from a remote machine to your own, you upload from your machine to another machine. What you upload can be a text file or a program that you want to share with others. Writers who are interested in on-line publishing or typesetting from their personal computers must have uploading capabilities. When you are sending or receiving data, your package may provide for error correction which will make sure that what you send is what the other computer gets, and vice-versa. Before you buy a communications package, consider what you will want to do once you go on-line.

There is a lot of good "public domain" communications software. Public domain software is software on which no one owns a copyright and which you can get free (for the price of a disk) from someone who already has it. One good way to find out about public domain software is to check with the users' group for your model of computer. For example, if you are buying or own a Commodore, get in touch with the Commodore Users' Group (which you can find out about from the dealer) and ask about free software. Members of users' groups are often heavily involved in developments that relate to their machines and keep up with all new packages that are made available. If there is a public domain package that does what you want, you can simply copy it onto a disk and have a software package free.

Public domain software is one very good reason to try to find a communications package that allows for downloading. Public domain software is not limited to communications. There are games, word processing, spreadsheet and many other kinds of free software available on networks, but you can only get a copy for your use if your communications software allows you to copy it while you are on-line.

One of the most widely used public domain communications packages is the MDM7xx (Modem7) program for machines using the CP/M operating system. First developed by Ward Christensen, Modem7 has been adapted by other people to run on a great variety of machines. Modem7 gives you many options as a networker, allows for both uploading and downloading and works with both acoustic and direct-connect modems.

If you can't find or don't want to look for public domain software, you can buy communications packages for any computer on the market. The prices range from $50 to $500.

Modems

A modem is the other piece of hardware that you will need for networking. A modem is a connector between your machine and the telephone lines. Modems come at various prices depending on their capabilities. There are two basic types of modems. One type, the acoustic coupler, is a little apparatus that you fit your telephone receiver into. (Incidentally, you must have a standard hand-set to work with acoustic couplers; weird shaped phones won't fit into the cups.) Rubber-like cups hold both ends of the phone securely and allow signals to pass back and forth between your computer and the phone lines. Acoustic couplers are limited as to the speed with which they can send data. They rarely exceed 450 bps (bits per second). The other type of modem is a small box into which the phone cord can be directly connected.

An acoustic coupler is less expensive than a direct-connect modem, more likely to pick up outside noise that can interfere with data transmission, and slower. The least expensive acoustic coupler modems are in the $50-$100 price range. Direct-connect modems range from $150 to $1500. The price gap between these two types of modem has narrowed greatly in the past few years, so that a direct-connect modem with its many options is not much more expensive than the basic acoustic coupler.

In addition to these two types of modem, there is also the possibility of having a modem built into your computer. This depends on the kind of machine you have.

You have other choices when you select a modem. Some modems send information at the rate of 300 bits per second (300 baud), others at both 300 and 1200 baud. Bits are the signals into which your computer translates your typed messages. There are eight signals which make up each letter, number or character. Each of these groups of signals is called a byte. That means that at 300 baud, you are sending and receiving about thirty characters a second. That's about as fast as you can comfortably read; however, if you are printing or copying files from another computer, 300 baud seems very slow. Most modems that transmit at 1200 baud send at 300 baud as well, so you can choose the rate of transmission depending on what you are going to do. Subscription information utilities often charge according to baud rate; 1200 baud is more expensive. If you intend only to hold conversations on a particular call, it is best to transmit at 300 baud. Most of us can't read any faster than that, and I don't know anyone who can type that fast.

You can also get modems that dial automatically, that remember the numbers of your favorite networks and connect you with them at the punch of a single button, that answer your phone and save information until you are ready to read it and that can do all those and more. Below is a list of features that are available on some modems.

Help command	Command modes
Command recognition	Command abort
Quit command	Manual dial
Dialing directory	Dial tones
Name selection dialing	Last number redial
Repeat dialing	Number linking
Directory modification	Auto-answer
Busy mode	Protocol detect and switch
Set answerback string	Set backspace character
Set attention character	Set disconnect character
Modem register contents	Modem switches
Built-in self-test	Infinite redial

You don't have to know what all this means, and you certainly don't need all these features to network, but at least you've heard the words and know there are a lot of choices.

A relatively new modem introduced by Visionary Electronics, the Visionary 1200, operates at either 1200 or 300 baud, contains up to 24 pages of battery-backed-up memory for sending, receiving and storing messages, has its own internal clock/calendar, and can send Telex and TWX messages. It is almost a little computer by itself. This modem will be used primarily by businesses that want the Telex feature, but depending on your interests, it might be just what you want. Prices for the Visionary 1200 range from $800 to $1,095, depending on the amount of storage space.

One of the most popular direct-connect modems is the Hayes Smartmodem. The Smartmodem comes in either 300- or 1200-baud models and has become so widely used that it is almost a standard. A number of micros can have the Smartmodem built into their serial interface card so that the communication port and modem become part of the machine. This modem can do almost anything you want and do it efficiently. When you are looking at hardware, look at various kinds of modems, compare price and features and keep in mind what you want to do. Remember, however, that the modem and software have to work together, as they do with your computer, so be sure that every piece of your system is compatible with the others.

There are other options available on the market for networkers. One clever little machine, the Scanset (from Tymshare, Inc.), is designed specifically for networking and information gathering. Called a personal information terminal, the machine has a phone, modem, autodialer and programmable function keys to get you where you want to be quickly and easily. Programmable function keys mean that you can make your machine understand that when you punch certain keys, it is supposed to dial up your favorite network or your sister Mary or get you into CompuServe. Scanset also provides both voice and data communications on the same line so that you can talk on the phone about what is appearing on the terminal. It operates independently of your computer when you want it to, or connects to your computer for transferring files. If you want to be on-line while your spouse is using the computer, this machine may be just what you need. It has a memory large enough to store most networking sessions, which can later be transferred to your computer or printer or thrown away, depending on how productive and interesting the evening was. Priced at about $895, it is a great deal more clever than most modems and costs two-thirds more. As networking becomes more popular, other new hardware will be designed to meet specific networking needs.

Shopping Tips

In the meanwhile, whatever hardware you choose will occasionally leave you with unanswered questions. This is one reason for shopping at a store where the employees are willing to help and answer questions in plain English. The best solution is to make friends with a technically oriented person. I've often wondered what I would have done without willing and patient experts. If you know someone who is a programmer or has good technical knowledge, by all means swallow your pride and ask for help. People are happy to share their expertise. Superiority is a heady feeling. If you don't have a technical friend, get in touch with the users' group for your computer. Most major brands have users' groups that meet regularly and discuss new applications, problems and tips specific to their machinery. Even if you don't care to participate regularly in the group, you can probably find someone to answer your questions.

Finally, make sure that you have all the information you need to hook up your equipment when you leave the store. Have the salesperson explain, repeatedly if necessary, how the modem attaches to the computer and to the phone and what you have to tell the software to make it all work together. Nothing is more frustrating than getting home with a new system and being unable to get it working. Never assume that you can figure it out from the instructions in the box—they are rarely clear, often written in technical jargon and sometimes not even there. Ask your salesperson to explain it slowly. Take notes. You might even try doing it yourself at the store before you try a solo venture at home. Even better, ask the dealer to deliver your machine, set it up and get you started. This is neither an uncommon nor unreasonable request, but something many stores do routinely. Also, feel free to call the store back in a few days or a few weeks whenever a problem appears that you can't handle alone.

The ideal computer store would have a policy of letting you take everything out on approval for a while to see how it all works and how well you like it. Regrettably, this is not the case. If it were, no one would ever buy a computer because there are so many out there to try. But be sure that before you buy you have an opportunity to spend some time in the store trying out the machine, figuring out how it works and making sure it does what you want. Computer dealers often have demo disks which they use to show what the machine can do. These are good to see, but do not take the place of your actually trying out the machine. The demonstration is designed specifically to make everything look easy, to show the machine to its best advantage and to convince you to buy. Rarely do things in real life work as smoothly as demos. Ask the salesperson to give you a few minutes alone with the machine after he or she has explained how it works and just experiment with different functions until you have a feel for it.

Once your decision is made, be sure that your dealer will be available to answer the questions that will inevitably arise when you put the machine into action, or at least find out if that is an option. If you buy a small machine from a toy or drug store, chances are good that you're going to be on your own from the beginning. If the salesperson is disgusted that you don't already know Pascal and the Christensen protocol, chances are good that you're going to get little useful help.

Actually, although computer salespeople are often abrasive, they are also sometimes genuinely knowledgeable and usually willing to help however they can. On the other hand, sometimes they don't know much about computers and have only memorized a bit of jargon. It is helpful to know which kind of salesperson yours is. The major problem lies in getting them to speak a language you can understand, and the only way to accomplish that is to continue repeating, "Please explain that in simple English," and "I want to use it, not redesign it."

3

Talk of the Town
Bulletin Boards

Electronic bulletin boards are a great way to begin electronic networking. True to their name, bulletin boards are free, are easily accessible and contain a hodgepodge of information. Generally, they are set up by individuals who run and maintain them as a hobby. Thus, they are also known as "hobby boards." There seems to be a propensity among computer enthusiasts to give everything initials or acronyms; thus, bulletin board systems are commonly known as "BBSs"—as in "Have you called your BBS today?" Bulletin boards are computer networks that are accessible by phone to anyone with a computer and modem. Anyone can become a part of the bulletin board network for the price of a phone call. The people who set up the bulletin board system are called "system operators" or "sysops" (pronounced sis' ops); it is their goal to provide entertainment, fun and information for themselves and anyone else who is interested.

Some Types of Boards

Joe, for example, is a graduate student in The University of Texas School of Music. After owning a computer for a while, he decided it would be fun to set up his own bulletin board. He bought the necessary software, and shortly thereafter, "The Diner" opened for business. Joe has created a complete scenario to make using his board more fun and more interesting for his users.

A typical trip to The Diner goes something like this: You dial the number and wait for an electronic tone to signal that the computer has answered. You then connect your phone to your modem and your printer or screen comes to life:

> "You've reached *****THE DINER***** Your waitress, Myrtle, comes over and asks you, 'Hon, what's your password?' (Or type the word 'new.')"

> [If you are a new user, the system will ask for your name or "handle" and assign you a password. You can now proceed.]

> "As you enter The Diner, you're met by your waitress, Myrtle. 'Hiya honey...How are ya? Sit yourself down, get comfy and read our menu.'"

The menu then appears on your screen and you are given choices of what you would like to do. That is the way The Diner begins. The varieties of bulletin boards are infinite. Some are designed to look like little towns, others like a poolhall.

You will find after some experimentation that boards have personalities very much like people. Some boards are very technically oriented—they cater to serious computerphiles. Most of their messages center around "bugs," "peripherals," "downloading" and such. There is a good bit of trading of both machinery, software and information on these boards. People buy and sell computer-related items and help each other out with technical questions and problems. Some of the postings you might see on this type of board include—

> "I am using Wordstar and my Epson MX80 printer. My problem is that when using underlining and boldface I get line 'creep' on my Epson. This is because Wordstar backspaces immediately after printing to underline or

boldface. Does anyone out there know of a way around this problem? Just drop me some mail. Any help or suggestions will be greatly appreciated."

"Tom, I heard that you've solved 'suspended.' I've got a problem with it. I can do everything except reset the filtering computer codes. I know that my problem is in replacing the wires in the FC channels, but I'm not sure how. Which cables should I replace, and with what?"

The people who leave these postings will get help with their problems, and anyone who reads the problems and solutions can also benefit from the information.

Another kind of board that is primarily computer-oriented is the "pirate board." These bulletin boards are usually engaged in illegal activities and therefore come and go and move around a lot—not unlike floating crap games. The purpose of these boards is to help people obtain free copies of copyrighted software and gain access to computers that are otherwise inaccessible. Many pirate board operators are young computer enthusiasts who enjoy the challenge of beating the system, of finding a chink in the software's armor that will allow them to copy it. Additionally, there is the thrill of getting software free rather than having to pay for it.

"Phone phreaking," a common pastime on pirate boards, is the charging of long-distance phone calls to someone else's phone number or to a secret account to which you do not have legal access. Phreaking can involve finding private long-distance codes—such as the ones used by MCI or SPRINT—and calling into computer systems in distant cities while charging the call to someone else's account. The codes are often discovered by having an automatic dialer run a program of random numbers until a valid identification number is hit. The phreaker doesn't know to whom the code belongs and doesn't care. Another way the random number program can work is by calling up a computer and trying random numbers until the computer is accessed. Once the codes are discovered, the phreakers pass them around among themselves and over pirate boards. This use of networking constitutes theft of service and is a punishable crime. Several young people have already been arrested for breaking into large computers owned by private industries and institutions. As networking becomes more common, harsher penalties will no doubt be imposed for pirating and phreaking.

Many other special interest groups get together around bulletin boards. There are boards that attract a large number of ham radio operators, for example. These boards provide a forum for exchanging information and a way to get to know people who share your interests. A growing technology of interest to ham operators is the ability to access on-line services by radio rather than phone lines. If you are a ham operator, you can check out this option by getting in touch with other operators using bulletin boards in your area. These examples of postings might appear on a ham network board—

"The amateur radio club meeting is held the second Tuesday of the month at 8 p.m. Listen for the ARO Swap Net on 46.94mhz every Sunday at 9 p.m."

"To celebrate Oman's Youth Year, A4XYY will be used in place of A4XRS as the headquarters station of the Royal Omani Radio Society for four days beginning November 18."

If ham radio or computers are your special interest, these bulletin boards will provide information you might have trouble finding anywhere else. Depending on your area, there may be other boards with emphasis on different topics. For the novice networker, however, general interest boards are usually the most fun and the most entertaining.

Almost any board you call will give you a choice of areas in which to browse and participate. There are main boards where people can post notices of general interest or introduce themselves to the group. One system operator describes his main board this way: "The main board is the one active when you first call. It contains most system news, general information and discussions on subjects not specifically covered on other boards. I ask people to watch their language on the main board because everyone has access to that one—even my grandparents who are real straight!"

Typical postings on the main board look like this—

"Hello to all of you. I am new on this board and would like to get some mail on this system."

"Anyone out there want to buy a Jeep cheap? I have a 1981 Suzuki 4WD Jeep in nice condition for $3000. Negotiable. Be the first one on your block to have one of these clever little Jeeps."

"Anyone interested in joining a new chapter of the Inventors Association should call 555-5555. The purpose of the group is to provide information and assistance to inventors in developing, patenting and marketing their inventions. Dues are $10. All are welcome."

One of the most-often-used features of local bulletin boards is E-Mail, or electronic mail. Although not all bulletin boards provide this service, many do. Users can leave private mail for other users and receive replies whenever they call into the system. Generally, people meet on the main bulletin board and then continue private conversations through the mail.

Bulletin board software is very flexible. It allows the system operator to set up any kind of board of interest to the group. He (at this point most sysops are men) can survey the group to find out what they'd like to see, or initiate new boards to check the responses, or simply put up the boards he likes and try to attract people with similar interests. Some examples of boards and typical listings follow.

MOVIE BOARD—informal reviews, by users of the system, of movies showing locally.

"Scarface is a typically fine Brian DePalma film. The action is hard-hitting and nonstop. Character development, set design, and fine acting by Al Pacino will make this movie a sure Oscar nomination bet. The only flaw is the ending, which leaves the viewer hanging. As one who has been in the same 'industry' as the character Tony Montana, I know that the research the director did was presented in a factual manner."

RESTAURANT BOARD—users' ratings and opinions of the best and worst places to eat in town.

"Jonathan's, on 54th Street, has added a new feature to the menu that is really terrific. On Thursdays, Fridays and Saturdays they have a seafood buffet—cold, hot, shrimp, oysters, clams, fish, lobster—all for $12.75 per person. It is usually crowded, so call and make reservations. Definitely worth the trouble."

STUDENT BOARD—this is especially popular in college towns where the boards are used as a way for students to get to know each other and exchange information about everything from professors to rock concerts.

"Hi, I'm an engineering student at the University, from Austria. Since I'm new in this country as well as this town, I'd like to get to know some people and find out what there is to do around here. I enjoy skiing, art museums and movies. Please get in touch if you'd like to be a tour guide."

ON THE TOWN—boards that cover local night spots and things to do when a user is ready to go out and do the town.

"Angels is opening again. This time with a bigger dance floor! This is a good club; last year they had killer drink specials seven days a week. Wednesday is the grand reopening party. Check it out."

MUSIC BOARD—this board is used to announce performances, concerts and events; to exchange, buy or sell tickets; and after the performance is over, to review the event.

"I have tickets to the Michael Jackson concert on the 17th which I have to sell. They are 35th row, center section. If you're interested, leave me a note."

ADULT BOARD—bulletin boards may call their adult section by various names, but most of them are explicitly sexual in nature and no holds are barred. Contributors are allowed to be as graphic as they like. Many of these boards require verification by the sysop that the user is an adult before he or she is allowed access to the board. I can't find any mild examples suitable for a general audience, so use your imagination or call up a local BBS with an adult board— but be warned: they are explicit!

48

GAMES BOARD—many different types of games are available on local bulletin boards. One of the most popular is an adventure game in which the player has to find the way out of a place by following clues, choosing items to carry along and trying to outwit various villains.

> "Welcome to the Games Board. You have just entered a wonderland of incredible choices and happy (and not so happy) endings. Somewhere near where you now stand is a treasure valued at more than $10 million. You are on a barren plain with only one hill in sight. At the base of the hill is a cave. On a sign near the entrance to the cave are these instructions: 'Take with you either a knife or a bow and enter here. If you get hopelessly lost, call for the Wise Old Man (WOM) and he will come to your aid.' Which do you choose—knife or bow?"

ISSUES AND IDEAS—this board is designed to let users voice their opinions on a variety of topics. Generally a user introduces a topic about which he or she has an opinion, and others are invited to add their ideas. The topic will remain the same until everyone interested has had an opportunity to speak; then someone else will bring up another idea. Often current events are discussed on these boards, or someone will recommend a book and discuss its importance. The sysop does not control the issues discussed, but may participate as one of the group.

> "I just finished reading *The Network Revolution* by Jacques Vallee. It is a fascinating look at the choices that society has regarding high technology. Although Vallee is a computer scientist, he writes in language that anyone can understand and talks about issues that affect us all. I highly recommend the book. I'd also like to hear others' reactions to the book, particularly regarding his distinction between 'data' and 'information.'"

SPECIAL INTEREST GROUPS—the subject of special interest groups is limited only by the interests of the people involved. As mentioned earlier, ham radio operators are one of many groups that use bulletin boards regularly. Other special interest groups—

gay activists, political action groups, musicians, IBM-PC users—
can be set up with the cooperation of the sysop.

STORY BOARD—budding authors practicing their craft, folks
who like to tell stories, and those who want to read stories by others
will enjoy the story board. Generally one person starts a story, writes
50 lines or less, then at some crucial point stops and lets someone
else pick up the story line. For some reason (probably because computer types are often science fiction fans) many of the stories are
science fiction. But they need not be; anyone can start any kind
of story, and anyone can change the course of the story in midstream.

" 'You must be the ones!' she shouted at them. 'Answer
me...did you hog the bathroom for the past ten days?'

"The guards dragged them down the hall and threw
them against the door until a small beady-eyed man
opened it.

" 'Vat hav ve heer?' spoke the man.

" 'What did he say?' asked Rufus.

" 'He said, "Vat hav ve heer," ' said the Wizard, who
was beaten on the head by the guards for his trouble..."

JOKES BOARD—as the name suggests, this board is simply a
joke exchange.

"There was this guy who was just crazy about
Beethoven. He had all the records that had ever been
made of his music; he had learned to play the piano just
so he could play Beethoven's pieces; he had even learned
to play everything Beethoven had ever written, but still
he wasn't satisfied. He decided that he had to have
Beethoven himself. So he travelled to Germany and began
digging up Beethoven's grave. He dug and dug, and finally
reached the coffin. Trembling with fear and anticipation,
the guy lifted the lid and looked into the coffin. He saw
Beethoven holding a manuscript in one hand and madly
erasing the notes with the other.

" 'What are you doing?' the guy asked.

" 'Leave me alone,' Beethoven said. 'Can't you see I'm
decomposing?' "

WOMEN ONLY—a sort of electronic back fence where women can talk to each other without male interference. Because so many networkers are currently men, these boards are set up to make women feel welcome and to give them a special place in the system. Usually, the sysop calls on a voice line to verify the gender of the user.

How to Join In

Using bulletin boards—regardless of the type of board that interests you—is exceedingly simple. All you need, aside from your equipment, is one phone number. As a service to users, most boards list the numbers of other bulletin boards. If you can't find an acquaintance to give you that first number, try calling a computer store in your area. The employees at such stores generally know what is going on electronically around town.

There are also several publications you can subscribe to that keep up with bulletin boards as they are added and dropped. *The On-Line Computer Directory,* created and published by Jim Cambron of Kansas City, Missouri, lists every bulletin board in the U.S. that Cambron can find. Cambron goes to great lengths to verify that the bulletin boards he lists are still in existence. The directory is published and mailed quarterly. For subscription information, contact J. A. Cambron Company, Inc., P. O. Box 10005, Kansas City, MO 64111, (816) 756-1847 or CompuServe: 70040,414.

The Computer Phone Book, by Mike Cane, published in 1983 by New American Library, is a good source for many numbers. Numbers are listed by geographical location and area of interest. An update to the book is available monthly for $20. This fact points out an important thing to remember about BBSs. They are usually run by one person working from his or her home and are likely to disappear or appear without warning. As a result, any printed list is somewhat out-of-date by the time you receive it. Still, the lists are very handy and can put you in touch with people you would otherwise have a hard time finding.

CompuServe and The Source are also avenues for finding BBS numbers. Each has a bulletin board section with notices pertaining to bulletin boards, networking and related topics.

The simplest and least expensive way, however, is to check with boards in your area. You can download or print their directories and make your calls from that list. Each time you call a new board you can check its list for additional boards. Some networkers call boards all over the country. Others limit their participation to local boards.

Each time you call a bulletin board, it will want to know who you are. If you have not called before, you type in "NEW," and the board will begin to explain itself. The following is a typical introduction to a board.

"If this is your first call to a Networks system, relax. It's one of the easiest computer dial-up systems to use. This section will give you the advice you need to get started.

"You have already done the hardest part, logging on. When you finish reading this you will be treated to the system news and the menu. The menu contains a short description of all the available commands. You are welcome to try any and all of them, but to get started, if you don't know what you're doing, you should select 'H' when the system asks you to choose a command. 'H' stands for 'help'. It is a detailed explanation of all the system commands. Two other good selections for the first-time caller are 'I' for 'information about the system' and 'J' for 'jargon,' which is a short dictionary of terms you will see used on this and other boards.

"Reading these options should take about 5 minutes, and you certainly don't have to read them. It's just good if you are having any problems. You are not required to do anything on the board, it's just here for you to have fun with.

"Don't worry, it'll get easy!! You cannot do any damage to the system over the phone, so feel free to play around. If you have any problems or questions, just leave a note for the sysop by selecting 'F' for 'feedback.' "

The first time you call, you will have to decide on a way to identify yourself on the board. Almost all boards require that you leave your real name with the sysop, but you can choose a "handle" for use on the board if you prefer. In some cases, this handle is also your password to get back on the next time you call. In other cases, the board will assign you a password, like SXP778d.

I've found it simpler to use the same handle on all boards. That way I can remember my name! In the case of boards that assign passwords, it is very handy to have a little notebook by your computer or terminal in which you write down the name of the board, its phone number and your password.

A handle allows you to remain anonymous on the board until you are ready to reveal your identity. In some cases, it's not a bad idea to choose whom you wish to know your name.

The password allows the computer to recognize you when you call again. The sysop wants to keep track of who is calling and weed out people from time to time who no longer use the board. That keeps his memory from being overloaded with inactive user information. The computer also has to be able to recognize you in case there is electronic mail for you (if the board has that feature).

Some sysops verify users before allowing them on the system. In these cases, you tell the board you are new; it asks your name and phone number, then tells you it will get back to you. The sysop calls to verify that you are who you say you are and gives you a password over the voice phone. Once you have your password, you are welcome to join the system.

Most bulletin boards have a section specifically designed for new users. This section describes the features of that particular board, tells you what your options are and instructs you in the commands you need to know to enjoy the board. The first time you enter a board it will probably be worth your time to read this information.

Using Menus

All of the boards are menu-driven. That means that you have a menu or list of choices to select from each step of the way. Menus are set up either numerically or alphabetically. For example, your choices may be listed on the screen as "A,B,C,D,E,F,G,?" The question mark means, "What is the menu? I don't know what these letters mean." In response to your "?" the board will list the menu:

     A—Apple Users' Group
     B—Bulletin boards

C—Chat with sysop

D—Download

E—Electronic mail

F—Feedback—leave a message for sysop

G—Goodbye (or sign off the system)

Generally, but not always, the letters correspond to words you can remember. The sysop can design his menu to please himself, and if he wants A to stand for Games, that's his prerogative.

Once you have made your choice from this menu, "B" for example, you may be given another menu to choose from: "1,2,3,4,5,6,?" Again you can ask for clarification by typing "?" The board will respond with—

1—General Interest Board

2—Adult Board

3—Story Board

4—Restaurant Board

5—Jokes Board

6—Game Board

Select your board, and you have another menu handed to you: "P,Q,R,S,T,?" Naturally, you type "?"

P—Post a bulletin

Q—Quit bulletin board

R—Read bulletins

S—Scan bulletins

T—Titles only

This may all sound long, drawn-out and complicated, but in fact the process takes only a few seconds, and once you become familiar with the board, you can skip the menu listings.

Let's assume you need a good laugh and have selected the Joke Board. You tell the board that you want to read the jokes.

The message comes up on your screen, "There are 43 active messages on this board. Read message #_____." You type in "42" and joke number 42 appears on your screen.

At this point you may decide to read a few more jokes, share a knee-slapper of your own or go play a game instead. If you decide to play a game, you work your way back using the same menus you used to get here: "Q" to quit, then "6" for Games.

Depending on the software the board uses and the preferences of the sysop, each board is slightly different. All, however, are easy to learn and offer abundant help for the novice user. As a last resort, you can leave a message for the sysop if you don't understand something.

The Sysop

Another bulletin board option is to "chat" with the system operator. This mode is the only way that you can talk directly with another person on a BBS. If you decide you want to talk with the person in charge rather than leaving him a message, you can select the "chat" option. The sysop's computer then signals that he is wanted. If he is not available, the computer tells you, "Sorry, the sysop can't chat now." If he is available, your conversation can begin. Unlike messages you post or mail you leave, there is no time delay in the chat mode. The sysop also has the option of instigating a chat.

Donald, sysop of a general interest board, spends a few minutes every evening monitoring the activity on his board. If someone new signs on while he's watching, he often interrupts to welcome the new user and ask if he or she has any questions about the board. Donald says, "After a few months, I feel I know the people who use my board. I get an idea of what they're interested in, what they like to do on the board, and sometimes when someone I recognize signs on, I jump in to say hello."

Generally, when the sysop wants to chat, he breaks into a likely spot with an announcement:

********ATTENTION PLEASE********
********THE SYSOP IS HERE!********

Sometimes you get the feeling that someone is watching over your shoulder when the sysop drops in. On the whole, however, the system operator is kept busy making sure that the board runs smoothly. It is no small task. Although most of the boards are hobby boards, they do require a good bit of time to maintain.

Many boards have a primary sysop who owns the machine and in whose home the machine lives, plus additional remote sysops. These people help out the sysop in a variety of ways—from developing new boards and maintaining them to filling in when the sysop is away for a few days. Sometimes a group of people will get together to share the responsibilities and costs of a bulletin board. Sysops are responsible for keeping the boards in operation, deleting old messages to make room for new ones, adding new boards or features and generally encouraging people to take advantage of all their hard work.

Downloading

One of the features that many boards offer is a download section. This means that you can call up and select from the board's offerings of free software. Software available on these boards is in the public domain or is developed by individuals who are not interested in commercializing their work. All of these programs are uncopyrighted (unless it is a pirate board), so there is no question of illegality involved. In fact, there is some very fine software that has been developed by hobbyists who are more than happy for other people to enjoy their creativity.

To copy software for your own use, you have to be sure that it is compatible with your machine. In the first place, you must have communications software that allows for downloading. If you use a dumb terminal or dumb-terminal software, you will not be able to download. See your software documentation to learn the procedure for your particular system. Once you have figured out how to download, you still must be sure that the program you are copying will run on your machine. If you are an Atari owner calling a board running on an Atari and want to download programs designed for Ataris, there is no problem. You select "Download" from the menu and the board tells you how to proceed. If you own a Kaypro and call a TRS-80 board to download an Apple program, you are in trouble. To be downloaded, a program need not be designed for your particular brand of machine, but it must be designed for your type of operating system. There are a great many different CP/M machines on the market, for example, and it is possible to download from one brand to another without a problem. It is not possible, however, to download from CP/M to MS-DOS without special software, and sometimes not even then. The best thing to do if you are not sure about compatibility is to ask the sysop for help and advice. He can generally tell you what is possible and what is not possible.

Many bulletin boards also hope that you will upload some of your own programs to the system library. If you are just a beginner, it is doubtful that you will have programs to contribute for a while, but if you do have public domain software or software that someone has developed for public use that is not already in the system, it is a good deed to upload it for others' use.

Your communications software documentation will tell you how to upload as well as download. Sometimes uploading is a little trickier because some packages require that the receiving machine have the same software as the sending machine. The quirks of your package will be detailed in the documentation.

Local Boards

Local bulletin boards are growing more popular daily, not only with computer buffs who have used them for several years, but with the general computer-owning population as well. They are ideally suited to the beginning user because, while they require no technical knowledge, they do allow for growth. As you become more familiar with your system and your favorite boards, your options will expand. Some boards have "Expert" sections for computer sophisticates to enjoy. Whatever your level of expertise, bulletin boards offer an inexpensive and enjoyable way to network.

Problems

The boom in networking, like most things, is not entirely positive. Most of the problems that have come from more and more people wanting to use bulletin boards, however, are minor. The biggest frustration for bulletin board enthusiasts is the busy signal. Most BBSs have only one phone line, so only one person can be on-line at a time. As more people call up the boards, the more difficult it becomes to get through. Generally the evening hours between five and midnight are the busiest, but some popular boards are difficult to get into at any hour. An automatic dialer can assuage this problem: the dialer calls the number again and again until it finally answers. It does not always allow you access whenever you wish, but it does save the tedium of dialing the number manually over and over.

Another problem is people who want to abuse rather than use the systems. These people try to figure out ways to break into the system, use other people's passwords, leave obscene or spurious messages and in general make the whole thing less pleasant for other users. As a result of this kind of vandalism, many sysops are opting for more stringent verification before allowing users access to the board.

Becoming a Sysop

For the most part, however, bulletin boards are easy, cheap and fun. That is their major function in life—to provide entertainment for both user and sysop. Most sysops began networking as bulletin board users. Todd says, "I moved to town and began calling up local boards as a way to meet people and find out what was going on in town. I learned about the Apple Users' Group from one of the boards and met a lot of people there. After a few months, I decided it would be really fun to start a bulletin board of my own. It was! I've had the board for about a year now and enjoy it more than ever."

In the event that you decide bulletin boards are such fun that you want one of your very own, there are a few things you should know. First, operating a bulletin board requires considerably more time and a bit more money than merely being a participant. To begin a basic bulletin board, all you really need is a communicating computer, an automatic-answering modem, bulletin board software and at least one disk drive. You probably will want another disk drive, a printer and a separate phone line for the computer.

Bulletin board software is available for most kinds of computers. There is even public domain software that can be used for bulletin boards. Probably the best way to decide which kind of software you'd like to have for your board is to look at other boards and find out what kind of software the one you like best uses. You must also find out if it will run on your machine. Remember, not only do the software and computer have to be compatible, the software and modem also have to be able to work together. It is possible to have a bulletin board that shares your regular phone line, but if you do, be warned that you will have limited time for getting calls since your board will probably keep the phone tied up most of the time. Remember, too, that while the board is in operation, your computer is also tied up.

Like most software, bulletin board software varies greatly in both features and price. You can get free software, but it may not be exactly what you want. You can also spend $350 for a package with a lot of bells and whistles. How much the system costs depends in great measure on how much you want it to do and how much you are willing to invest in it.

Strange Questions

Whether you decide to start your own bulletin board or just enjoy someone else's, you definitely should give them a try. If you are a true novice, here are a couple of questions that may throw you the first time they appear on your screen:

How many nulls? Nulls are pauses in the information sending pattern. If you are using a printer or an old terminal or some other type of machinery that needs a breather between lines to get its act together, you may need some nulls. Check your documentation to be sure, but most computers do not require nulls. Even the old communicating, printing terminal I had when I began did not require nulls.

Do you require line feed? That's the one my old printer did need. Again, you have to check your documentation to find out if your machine needs to be told when one line ends and another begins. As you'll find out, if a machine needs line feed and you say it doesn't, you end up with all lines printed on top of the first, which makes reading extremely difficult.

Can you accept lower case? Some computers print both lower- and upper-case letters; others can handle only upper case. This makes a difference to the sending computer. Each of these questions has a simple answer, once you check the information that came with your computer, terminal or word processor. Usually, once a BBS asks you the questions, it stores the data and never has to ask again. Some BBS software, however, has to ask you every time you call. In either case, you have only to look it up once. Anything else you need to know, the bulletin board will tell you. Some BBSs ask you what kind of computer you have, others want to know various other kinds of information, but primarily they ask your name and city of origin.

Computer bulletin boards have been around since 1978, when Ward Christensen and Randy Suess of Chicago designed a system for local computer club members to leave messages for each other. This original board has spawned the hundreds that now prosper across the country—and is still in operation at (312) 546-8086.

In addition to general interest boards, there are a growing number of special interest boards. A board in West Palm Beach, Florida, was set up specifically to meet the needs of freelance writers. Medical boards serve as places for doctors and others in the medical field to share information and expertise. Education boards are a place for educators and interested parties to share opinions and methods. Religious boards allow people with like beliefs to get together. There is no reason at all why any topic of interest to people would not be a suitable topic for a bulletin board. In *The Computer Phone Book,* BBSs are listed by field of interest as well as geographic area.

Whether you want someone to talk to at 2 a.m. when the neighbor's dog is entertaining you with his version of the "Warsaw Concerto," or to buy a printer for your new computer system, or to find out where the single swingers' club meets, or to learn what that new Chinese restaurant is like, a local bulletin board is a good place to begin looking. Bulletin boards can provide you with information you need for work or for your favorite hobby, or they can find you a friend—maybe that special someone in your life. At the very least, they can provide you with both entertainment and experience in networking with your computer or word processor.

4

Calling New York, Paris, Pasadena—Let's Talk!

Information Utilities

Once your appetite for communicating electronically has been whetted by local bulletin boards, you will probably want to expand your network. Local BBSs are fun and helpful but, for the most part, limited by the ages and interests of the participants and by the software's limited functions.

You are ready to move on to the big wide world of information utilities. Information utilities are large computer centers filled with huge, powerful computers, which in turn are filled with zillions of pieces of information and lots of possibilities. All this is available to the electronic networker—to you, with your communicating machine.

CompuServe and The Source are the two largest information utilities in the United States. There are many others with varying amounts of data, but these two are easily used for networking. Information utilities are also called videotex, a term generally used to describe services that display text and graphics on remote video screens.

Videotex, originated in Great Britain in the early 1970s, is very popular in Europe today. Both Britain and France have large videotex services. The system was originally designed for people to call in and have the big computers give them information on their screens at home. As the system is commonly used in Europe, data are sent to videotex subscribers through their home television sets. The subscribers use a videotex terminal—a small box with numbers on it—to request data. This is a useful function of the utilities, but it is certainly not their only, or even their most valuable service.

The Source

The Source, located in McLean, Virginia, began in 1979 as the Telecomputing Corporation of America. In 1980 Reader's Digest bought the company and changed its name to Source Telecomputing Corporation. The facility consists of twelve Prime 750 minicomputers. When The Source started, people called in and got messages in their electronic mailboxes, read news items and got information from databases.

David Hughes, of Colorado Springs, signed on and wondered about the other people who were using the system. He left a message on the bulletin board saying something to the effect of "Is anybody out there? I seem to be caught in a void." The result was overwhelming. David got message after message from people who wanted to talk to other people rather than to machines. After some 600 messages, the SourceVoid movement was begun. David has pioneered in several areas of electronic networking, not the least of which was the personal networking potential of The Source.

David Hughes is a nontechnical person who had the imagination and chutzpah to strike out in new directions that technical folk had not even considered. A lover of language and former English teacher, David realized that electronic communication was a powerful new way for people to contact each other. According to David, the information utilities thought they were selling information, but in fact they were selling communication and didn't even know it.

David and his fellow Source subscribers began to form networks.

Discussions sprang up around many different topics, interests were revealed and a whole new way of using the system evolved. One of the best things about the large utilities is that the company provides the equipment, and the users are relatively free in how they use it. Both The Source and CompuServe are open to suggestions and proposals for new features.

The Source currently offers over 700 features and programs for subscribers, including six different specifically communications-centered options. To take advantage of these opportunities, you have to become a subscriber. You can join The Source by purchasing a start-up package at your local computer store. More than likely the place where you bought your equipment can get you started on The Source. You can also contact The Source directly at their customer support number, (800) 336-3330 (in Virginia, (800) 570-2070).

As you might expect, when you get a lot more stuff, you have to pay more money. Costs, however, are very reasonable considering the power and flexibility of The Source. There is a one-time charge of $49.95 when you subscribe to The Source. Once you pay your $49.95, you receive the manual, an ID number and a password to allow you on the system, The Source command guide, a subscription to *SOURCEWORLD Newsletter,* a customer-support hotline phone number, and on-line access to The Source. To connect with The Source, you call a local Telenet or Tymnet number. Telenet and Tymnet are operations that send information over phone lines from one place to another. Although they add surcharges to the call, they are generally cheaper than long-distance calls. The general rate for Telenet or Tymnet calls is $2 to $10 per hour, depending on the time of day. You can check with your local phone company to make sure you're using the least expensive route. Rates for The Source are $20.75 an hour from 7 a.m. to 6 p.m. daily and $7.75 an hour from 6 p.m. to 7 a.m. and on weekends and holidays. Almost all utilities base charges on the time at the location at which you are billed. Outside the continental U.S., rates are slightly higher. This rate is for a 300-baud modem. If you have a 1200-baud modem, the rates increase to $25.75 and $10.75, respectively. There is also a minimum monthly charge of $10 whether you use the system or not. This monthly charge includes approximately two double-spaced pages of free storage.

The Source estimates that the average monthly charge for users is $25. Of course, that can vary widely depending on how much you use the system. Once you get started talking to people and looking around the system, it's easy to lose track of the time and run up a terrific bill. The Source bills only through major credit cards—American Express, Visa and MasterCard. Corporate members may apply for direct billing.

With 700 options to choose from, decisions are not easy. However, most people have their favorites and spend most of their time using the same areas again and again. For networkers, the communications section is the most valuable. The Source offers several different ways that you can connect with other people.

SOURCEMAIL is the version of electronic mail provided by The Source. It allows you to exchange mail almost instantaneously with anyone on the system. It also lets you send many copies of the same letter quickly and efficiently. Many small businesses are using Sourcemail for their direct marketing efforts. People who want to get in touch with others who share their interests also use Sourcemail to make contact and carry on remote correspondence.

MAILGRAM Message Service allows you to send actual Mailgrams—messages on paper—to people who are not members of the system. Next-day delivery is guaranteed. The U.S. Postal Service's E-COM is also a part of this service, allowing rapid delivery of mail that is created and sent electronically, then delivered in paper form.

COMPUTER CONFERENCING lets you talk directly with people all over the country. Many businesses use the conferencing function to bring salespeople together for sales meetings regardless of where they happen to be at the time.

CHAT offers direct, real time communication with another person.

BULLETIN BOARDS let you post messages to the whole community of subscribers to The Source. Your audience is much greater than on local bulletin boards.

MEMBER DIRECTORY lets you get in touch with other subscribers who share your interests. For example, you can tell the computer to search the directory for people who have listed spelunking as an interest. You will receive their names and Source addresses.

PARTI (short for Participate), the conferencing mentioned above, features ongoing conferences on a variety of subjects. PARTI lets any subscriber start a conference by choosing a subject. Other subscribers can then call in and add their comments. The result is often a wide variety of opinions and outlooks on a broad base of topics. All the information is stored on The Source, so you can catch up on what was said while you were away.

When you subscribe to The Source, you are given a user identification number and a password, and you are assigned to a specific computer system, such as System 10. You need to know all three of these things when you sign onto The Source. After you place your call, the computer will ask you for them.

There are two ways of moving about in The Source. One is the traditional menu method that you learned by using local bulletin boards. The other is called Command Level. Command Level is quicker once you learn the proper commands, but Menu is simpler. If you want to join a group discussion using the Menu commands, your trip will look something like this:

WELCOME TO THE SOURCE

1 USING THE SOURCE
2 TODAY
3 BUSINESS UPDATE
4 THE SOURCE MAIN MENU
5 COMMAND LEVEL
ENTER ITEM NUMBER OR HELP 1
You then enter your choice: "4."

THE SOURCE MAIN MENU

1 NEWS AND REFERENCE RESOURCES
2 BUSINESS/FINANCIAL MARKETS
3 CATALOGUE SHOPPING
4 HOME AND LEISURE
5 EDUCATION AND CAREER
6 MAIL AND COMMUNICATIONS
7 CREATING AND COMPUTING
8 SOURCE*PLUS
Your choice here is "6."

(By the way, SOURCE*PLUS offers features which can be used for additional fees.)

MAIL AND COMMUNICATIONS

1 MAIL

2 CHAT

3 POST

4 PARTICIPATE

5 MAILGRAM MESSAGES

ENTER ITEM NUMBER OR HELP P

To Participate, you type in "4."

At this point, the computer will tell you what discussions are going on, how many are participating and how to get into a discussion.

If you select "5" at the first menu, you will automatically go into the Command Level. Commands are issued by typing in one of the key words listed in your users' manual and command guide. To issue a command, you first type in a prefix word indicating what you want the program to do. For example, if you type "INFO" as your prefix, the computer will give you information and background material about your topic. If you say "INFO PARTI," you will receive information about ongoing conferences. Assistance for each of the key words is available by typing "HELP" and the key word. Within each key word section are additional commands to select the operations you want. Probably because it is more expensive than CompuServe and because it is available 22 hours a day, The Source has evolved into a service used more for professional purposes than for general fiddling around. Many small and midsized businesses use The Source because it provides all they need for a lot less money than installing a network of their own. Conferencing is especially popular among sales forces spread all over the country. The head of the sales department can call a meeting of salespeople for Tuesday morning at 9:30 to discuss the month's revenues. The boss calls The Source from the office and enters the conference option. Harry, in Pittsburgh, calls from home to join in; Janice, in a hotel in Akron, uses her portable computer to dial in; Mary calls in from a public phone in the airport in Los Angeles. Compared with the cost of flying in and housing all these people or of buying a large computer and a network to connect them with the home office, the charges from The Source are negligible.

There is business, and there is *business*. Many of us have vocations and avocations, and sometimes it is hard to tell which are the most time-consuming and important in our lives. My business is working for a software corporation, and when someone asks who I am with, I automatically say "Execucom." My *business*, however, is communication. Whether writing a book or a poem or a short story or talking with people on the phone or the computer, what I really want to do is communicate. So I don't conduct official business through networks, but I certainly conduct my *business* through networks.

Then there is "business" business and personal business. Floyd is a pharmaceutical salesman in his business life, but he keeps track of his personal finances and his hobby of collecting vintage phonograph records electronically. He can use the facilities of The Source to manage his finances and contact people who share his interest in records and who are possible sources of new additions to his collection. Floyd buys and sells records, so in a sense, it is a business effort; but primarily it is a labor of love. More than the money involved, he enjoys talking to people who share his enthusiasm, and it is much easier to find those people through The Source than in the course of his daily visits with doctors and hospitals or even through local bulletin boards, since it is not an enthusiasm shared by great numbers of people.

CompuServe

CompuServe is the other major information utility and communication network in the United States. CompuServe is located in Columbus, Ohio, and is a division of H & R Block. In early 1984, CompuServe welcomed its 100,000th subscriber, and the number is growing by leaps and bounds. During the daytime hours, CompuServe's computers are involved in Block business and are generally not accessible by subscribers. For that reason, CompuServe is sometimes called "the nighttime utility." CompuServe is accessible during "prime time" on an as-available basis (8 a.m.-6 p.m.), and the rates are higher then. Subscriptions are available from your computer store for a sign-up fee of $19.95. You can also contact CompuServe directly between 9 a.m. and 9 p.m. eastern time at (800) 848-8199. (In Ohio call (614) 457-8650.) If you subscribe to

CompuServe through your computer store, you get a package containing a valid password and user identification number and, sometimes, a free hour or two to look over the service before signing on. This enables you to begin using the service immediately. If you sign up through the customer service department, it may take several days to get your password.

As with The Source, you can call into CompuServe by making a local phone call. CompuServe, however, has established a large network of its own which allows you to call without the extra charges for Telenet and Tymnet. When you receive your packet of information from CompuServe, there will be a list of cities and their phone numbers you can call direct. The list is constantly being added to, so if your town is not already on the list, it might pay to check periodically to see if it has been added.

Rates for CompuServe are $6 per hour for Standard Service—6 p.m. to 5 a.m. weekdays, all day Saturdays, Sundays and announced holidays—and $22.50 per hour for Prime Service. If you are transmitting at 1200 baud, the rates increase to $17.50 and $35 respectively. There is no monthly minimum charge for Standard Service, but a two-hour monthly minimum for Prime Service. Prime Service is an option available by contract only after Standard Service is established.

Included in your subscription is 128,000 characters of storage space. Additional storage space can be rented for $4 per week per 64,000 characters. Your CompuServe charges can be billed to Visa or MasterCard accounts, or direct billing can be arranged. One of CompuServe's direct billing options is called "Checkfree." Under this system, you receive a bill for your service and a date that your bank will make a payment from your checking account. It is similar to direct withdrawals for insurance or other payments. There is no charge by CompuServe or the bank for this option.

CompuServe, like other utilities, gives you a password when you subscribe. They recommend that you change your password from time to time to ensure that no one else discovers it and begins charging time to your account. Almost all utilities maintain privacy by encoding passwords in the computer; therefore, it is very important that you remember your password. If you lose or forget it, you will have to apply for a new one, since no one can find out what your original password was.

CompuServe's networking options are similar to those The Source offers. There is an electronic mail option that notifies you immediately after you sign on if you have mail waiting. Also, there are several public bulletin board options for leaving messages.

There are other ways that you can use CompuServe to communicate with other people. One of the most popular is the CB Simulator. Like CB radios, the CB Simulator lets many people talk together at one time. People sign in with a "handle" and talk back and forth with other CBers. There are several different CB channels going at the same time; CompuServe lets you know how many people are talking on each channel. If an especially interesting conversation develops between two people, they may switch to a private channel to carry on their talk. Many people have met and developed lasting friendships through CB.

The CBers have developed their own little network, complete with gossip columnist, etiquette, special interest group and newsletters. There are a variety of options for communication within the CB network as well. If you want to have a really private conversation, you can select the /SCRAMBLE option to encode your transmissions so that only the person you are sending to can read them. A list of commands is available by typing "H" for help.

Communication through CB is immediate; that is, everyone is on the channels at the same time, calling and responding as they would in a CB radio conversation. Unlike local bulletin boards, the large utilities allow real time conversations that don't require you to call back later to see if someone has answered your message.

Another area on CompuServe that allows real time communication is the Special Interest Groups or SIGS. There are more than fifty SIGS on CompuServe; within each is the option of conferencing. People can go to the topic area that interests them and join others for a conversation. Many SIGS have regularly scheduled conference times, including times when an expert on the subject is available to answer questions and contribute to the discussion. Within each SIG is a sysop who moderates the discussion and keeps things moving along.

The sysop is also responsible for the SIG message section—a bulletin board. Records of conferences with visiting celebrities are also kept so that those who were not able to attend can catch up with what was said. Each Special Interest Group has an area of disk storage for recording conversations or programs. Much public domain software is stored in this area; users are welcome to download the programs and use them on their home computers.

Most of the SIGs are found in the Home Services section or the Services for Professionals section. If you type "GO HOM-50" at the first "!" prompt, you will get a list of discussion groups in the Home Services section:

COMPUSERVE PAGE HOM-50
DISCUSSION FORUMS

1 CBERS	10 LITERARY
2 HAMNET	11 EDUCATORS
3 NETWITS	12 ARCADE
4 ORCH 90	13 GAMES
5 SPORTS	14 FAMILY MATTERS
6 COOKING	15 GOOD EARTH
7 TRAVEL	16 WORK-AT-HOME
8 SPACE	17 MUSIC
9 ISSUES	18 FOOD BUYLINE

19 INSTRUCTIONS
20 DESCRIPTIONS
DISCUSSION FORUMS (CONT.)

1. ANIMAL & PET CARE
2. ENTERTAINMENT
3. RELIGION
4. SKI FORUM
5. OUTDOOR FORUM

If you have a system that allows it, it's a good idea to download these most-often-used menus and print them out so that they are handy when you're planning your next visit to the system. The description of each forum is also a good thing to print and keep on hand.

In the Services for Professionals area, there are SIGs for a great variety of vocations and avocations. Typing "GO SFP" will get you the list of choices.

As in other sections, each SIG offers a bulletin board, regularly scheduled meetings and special features. All the SIGS are open without charge to any subscriber of CompuServe. Whether your interests are professional or purely for your own enjoyment, there is a wealth of information and expertise just waiting to be tapped in the special interest groups.

Another real-time communication option on CompuServe is in the Games area. Some of the game options are discussed in Chapter 5.

To enter CompuServe, you use the same general procedure as when calling a local bulletin board. You dial a local number—either CompuServe, Telenet or Tymnet—and wait for the screaming tone on the other end of the line that signals connection has been made with a computer. If you use an acoustic modem, put your handset in the modem. If you use a direct-connect modem, it will automatically connect your terminal to the computer. If you called Telenet or Tymnet, you will have to tell it which service you are calling. If you called CompuServe direct, the computer will tell you "CONNECT." You hold down the control key while you type "C" to let it know you are there. The computer then asks for your user identification number. "USER ID" is your cue to type in the number you have been issued. The computer will check to make sure it is a valid ID number and, assuming it is, will then ask for your password. Sometimes the validation takes a while, so don't give up. Type your password in carefully because it will probably be invisible on your screen. You have more than one chance to enter your password, but if you get it wrong several times, you will be automatically cut off. Once you have been cleared to enter the system, CompuServe will then identify itself and tell you the time and date of your call.

When you first sign onto the network you are given some options about what appears on your screen. If you wish, you can read your mail first and then get on to other business. If you have no mail, you will get a series of announcements about what's new on the system. These are brief notices; you can get more detail about things that interest you by typing "GO NEW" at the "!" prompt. CompuServe's main prompt is the exclamation point. Each system has its own symbol to tell you that it's your turn to make a choice. A prompt can be a colon, an arrow, or any other symbol, but in any case it is your signal to type in a command. If you do not see the prompt, whatever you type will usually be ignored by the system. Sometimes you have to hit the "Enter" or "Return" key to finish whatever you are doing before you will see a prompt.

Two commands to remember are "HELP" and "?." You can type these on almost any system and get assistance.

Once the announcements have been made, you are usually presented with the main menu. This menu allows you to select from the major sections of the network. As with many bulletin boards, you will be presented a series of menus from which you make choices and narrow down your field of interest. Once you know more about the system and what you want to do, you can skip the menus and go directly to your destination by using the GO command. Help messages are available all along the way in case you get lost or need further information.

CompuServe's information is divided into pages 32 characters wide by 12 lines long. Along with your subscription to CompuServe you will receive *CompuServe Highlights*, a guide to many available services, *Update Magazine*, and a complete subject index. This index lists topics and the commands needed to get there. An on-line index, accessed by "GO IND-54," will tell you page numbers for each topic. For example, if you are interested in checking out the CB Simulator, once you are given the "!" prompt and type in "GO CB" you will be in the CB area.

There are seven major sections of CompuServe:

```
1 HOME SERVICES
2 BUSINESS & FINANCIAL
3 PERSONAL COMPUTING
4 SERVICES FOR PROFESSIONALS
5 USER INFORMATION
6 INDEX
7 REDUCED HOLIDAY RATES
!
```

When you see this menu you will have three choices. You can type "H" (for help) and receive more information about the categories; you can type a number to indicate your selection; or you can type a direct command like "GO TWP-12," which means you need some financial advice. If you follow the menu route, your journey from the top menu to the CB simulator will look like this:

COMPUSERVE PAGE CIS-1
COMPUSERVE INFORMATION SERVICE
1 HOME SERVICES
2 BUSINESS & FINANCIAL
3 PERSONAL COMPUTING
4 SERVICES FOR PROFESSIONALS
5 USER INFORMATION
6 INDEX
7 REDUCED HOLIDAY RATES
ENTER YOUR SELECTION NUMBER, OR H FOR
MORE INFORMATION
! Enter your choice: "1."

COMPUSERVE PAGE HOM-1
HOME SERVICES
1 NEWS/WEATHER/SPORTS
2 REFERENCE LIBRARY
3 COMMUNICATIONS
4 HOME SHOPPING/BANKING
5 GROUPS AND CLUBS
6 GAMES AND ENTERTAINMENT
7 EDUCATION
8 HOME MANAGEMENT
9 TRAVEL
LAST MENU PAGE. KEY DIGIT OR M FOR
PREVIOUS MENU
! Your turn again; type in "3."

COMPUSERVE PAGE HOM-30
COMMUNICATIONS
1 ELECTRONIC MAIL
(USER-TO-USER MESSAGES)
2 CB SIMULATION
3 NATIONAL BULLETIN BOARD
(PUBLIC MESSAGES)
4 USER DIRECTORY
5 TALK TO US
6 LOBBY LETTERS OF AMERICA
7 ASK AUNT NETTIE
8 CB SOCIETY

LAST MENU PAGE. KEY DIGIT OR M FOR PREVIOUS MENU

! You are finally there—almost. "2."

Once you reach the CB section, you have a few more choices:

CB INFORMATION PAGE CB-10
CITIZENS BAND SIMULATOR
1 INSTRUCTIONS
2 CB ETIQUETTE
3 CB BAND A (MAINFRAME A)
4 CB BAND B (MAINFRAME B)
5 CBIG SPECIAL INTEREST GROUP
6 CB SOCIETY: CUPCAKE'S COLUMN
7 COMPUTING ACROSS AMERICA
LAST MENU PAGE. KEY DIGIT OR M FOR PREVIOUS MENU

! "3."

Now you have really reached your goal. (Band A is the original CB channel, but the area is so popular that Band B has been added to take care of all the users. You can take your choice. I chose "3.")

Once you have chosen the desired band, you will be cautioned not to reveal your password or to use obscene language (under penalty of fine and suspension of service). You will also be asked to pick a handle by which your CB pals will know you. A current listing of channels in use and the number of users tuned to each will let you know how many people are talking in each place. The number in parentheses is the channel number; the number after it tells how many users are there:

(Channel) users tuned in
(1) 13, (2) 7, (3) 9, (4) 18, (5) 2 Which channel: (You choose.)

Once you select your channel, you are dropped into the middle of the chatter (channel number and handle are in parentheses before each comment):

(A4, TWINKLETOES) I'm leaving cause I'm being ignored.
(A4, CAREBEAR) Don't leave, Toes, I'll talk.
(A4, BOZO) Hi all, I'm from Toronto.

And on and on and on. Whatever you type shows up on the screen with your handle preceding it. Commands must be preceded by a "/" and will not be seen by other CBers. Whenever you are ready to leave, all you have to do is type "/EXI" and you will exit the CB Simulator. The publications that come with your subscription are invaluable in keeping you up to date on the system and helping you find what you are interested in. Although it's a lot of fun to wander aimlessly around the large utilities, you have to keep in mind that in this case time really is money.

When you are planning to use any of the utilities, unless you don't care how much it costs, you really should have a plan before you pick up the phone. By spending a little time looking through the aids for users that the companies provide, you can save a lot of money. If you write down beforehand how to get where you want to go, you can save precious computer time by going directly there. After all, what you want to do is participate, not just meander through. At least that's what you want to do most of the time.

Also, if you are using the utilities for sending mail or leaving messages or questions, it's a good idea to write down what you have to say before you get on the system. That way you say just what you want to say, you don't feel time-pressured when you are composing, and you don't waste money.

There are several information utilities available besides CompuServe and The Source. Many of them, however, do not make communication one of their options. Although some have electronic mail as part of their service, they are generally designed as data retrieval services rather than communication media.

Delphi

One system that does include communication options is Delphi. Located in Cambridge, Massachusetts, Delphi is owned and operated by General Videotex Corporation. Begun in February, 1983, this system is offering some competition to the two larger services. Delphi charges a lifetime membership fee of $49.95 to enter the system. You receive a handbook, updates to the handbook, and a subscriber newsletter, and you get your first hour on the system free. Service during office hours, 8 a.m. to 6 p.m. weekdays, is $16 per hour; the rates go down to $6 per hour at other times. Delphi charges no minimum use fee, nor does it charge additional rates for 1200-baud modem use. Fees can be charged to American Express, MasterCard or Visa. The first 25,000 characters of storage is free; the charge for each additional 1,000 characters per month is five cents. Some of the services on Delphi have additional charges. The same is true on other networks. Whenever an option costs more than the basic connect charge, a system will let you know by placing "$" before the selection. For information or to sign up with Delphi, you can contact the Customer Information Service at (800) 544-4005 (in Massachusetts (617) 491-3393). To access Delphi, you call a local Tynmet or Telenet number.

Delphi offers most of the features of the two larger information utilities. Among these offerings are:

APPOINTMENT CALENDAR - the service will provide you with a program to keep track of your meetings and appointments. It will even remind you of important events without your having to look at the appointment book.

BULLETIN BOARDS - post, read and reply to messages from other members of the system.

DIRECT COMMUNICATION - the system will tell you who is on-line when you are and let them know if you are interested in chatting.

DEAR ORACLE - a section designed to allow users to get advice on just about anything from other members with special skills. You can also volunteer your own expertise here.

INFOMANIA - an open section where members publish their writing, design polls, collaborate on novels, and anything else they can think of.

MAIL - private exchange of messages with members of Delphi and the ability to send mail to subscribers of The Source, CompuServe and other services.

Delphi's big selling point is user friendliness. Have you heard that before? In this case, it's true. The commands are in English— "Library, Appointment Calendar, Add, Change," etc. There are also numerous, clearly written help messages, which explain rather than simply relisting commands.

The first time you sign on to Delphi you will be given a guided tour of the system. The "guide" explains the various sections of the system and how to move around within the system, then lets you visit each system briefly. Once the tour is completed, you're ready to venture out on your own. The tour is very helpful, and directions are easy to understand. You may want to download or print the tour to have it handy the next time you call in to Delphi.

There are several ways of making contact with other people through the Delphi system. As in any other system, the bulletin boards are an easy way to learn about other users and their interests and activities. If you're looking for people with specific interests or traits, the User Profile section lets you search through user information by entering any of up to 100 key words. For example, if you're looking for someone who plays tennis, jogs, and is a firefighter, you can type in those three words and the computer will find the people who fit your description. User information is voluntarily entered by each user, so you can remain anonymous if you wish.

Delphi also offers a Conference mode that is somewhat different from that of the other utilities. When you select Conference from the menu, you are given several choices. One of your options is to ask the computer "Who?" The system will then tell you who is on-line at that moment. If you see someone you'd like to talk with, you can send that person a message and a beep to meet you in the conference section. If that is mutually agreeable, the conversation can begin. If, however, you wish to work undisturbed, you can tell the system, and you won't be bothered.

Announcements of regularly scheduled conferences on various topics are made on the bulletin boards. Spontaneous conferences also go on frequently, and newcomers are welcome to join.

Another enjoyable feature of Delphi is the Collaborative Novel section. Several novels are in progress at all times, and users are welcome to add their contributions. Once a novel has reached some sort of conclusion, it is transferred to the Author's area where users can read it at their leisure.

Polling is another option on Delphi. You can write up a survey on any topic and ask for responses from other users. Some of the surveys are business-related, others are opinion polls about general topics, and some are just for fun. In any case, polling is a wide-open field you can use however it is most helpful to you.

Delphi is making a heavy push to attract special interest groups and clubs to the system. It is the home of the *Space Research Newslet-*

ter. Designed for people in aerospace research and related businesses, the newsletter includes bibliographies of research reports, analyses of space experiments, updates on political developments, news of conferences, classified ads for professionals and businesses, and much more. This newsletter and others like it are available at extra cost to Delphi subscribers. The developer of the special interest group serves as a sort of sysop for that area and can expand his or her area as needed.

Delphi is a new system, which is a benefit to its users since, while offering most traditional utility options, it is also expanding and wide open to suggestions. One of the things that the marketing brochure stresses is that you can be "a part of the design committee." Delphi is eager to find out what users want in a utility and to try to provide it.

Dow Jones

The Dow Jones News Retrieval Service is a large information utility specifically designed for people interested in business and financial news. Located in Princeton, New Jersey, DJNS, as it is referred to by friends, is strictly oriented toward financial news and information. The news is drawn from the *Wall Street Journal*, *Barron's*, and other news services. Included are more than eighty news categories and information on over 6,000 companies in diverse industries.

Stock quotes direct from the trading floors of the New York Stock Exchange and the American Midwest and Pacific exchanges are available after the required fifteen-minute delay.

News is immediate and is kept on the system for ninety days after being listed. Movie reviews, world news, sports reports and weather data are also available. More information about Dow Jones is included in Chapter 10.

The least expensive rates for access to DJNS range from $9 to $72 per hour depending on which feature you are using. Initial subscription cost is $50. DJNS is one of the hardest utilities to estimate costs on since the prices of features vary greatly and discounts are offered on some items. For more information, contact Dow Jones at (800) 257-5114 (in New Jersey, (609) 452-1511).

Many other information utilities are listed in Chapter 11. Their primary function is to provide data rather than channels of communication.

For networking, The Source, CompuServe, and Delphi are perfect. They give you many options, can be tailored to fit your needs and pocketbook, and are simple enough to be enjoyable to use. Once you begin using the systems, you'll wonder how you ever got along without them.

5

Fun and Games in the Electronic Age

Games and Entertainment

As any five-year-old can tell you, playing with someone else is usually more fun than playing by yourself. There are zillions of games out there that you can play on your computer. And they are fun. Just step into a video arcade sometime and you will see all sorts of people having a good time playing games with machines. But what if, like that five-year-old, you are tired of playing with your toy all by yourself?

Electronic networking makes it possible to enjoy a variety of fun things with other people. In the first place, every time you play one of those games in a video arcade, you have to feed money into the machine. If you buy home video games, you have to buy a control box and then buy a cassette for every new game you want to play. If you play on your communicating machine, however, you don't have to pay much of anything.

Many local bulletin boards have game sections. In these sections you can find games that you can play on-line and games that you can download to your own machine to play whenever you want. A very popular bulletin board game is Adventure. This game involves working yourself around in a maze, picking up various items to help you reach your goal and finding a treasure or being eaten by a monster. If you live in a town with a bulletin board that offers such games, you can play absolutely free. If you call up an out-of-town board, you will have to pay long-distance charges. In either case, you can enjoy the game without having to buy a game unit or additional software.

The Source, CompuServe and Delphi offer the opportunity to play many more games, some of them with other people. Delphi has no formal multi-player game section so far, but there are some user-operated games which you may enjoy. Usually there are postings on bulletin boards about games that are going on. You simply contact the person running the game and find out what to do to play. One active game on Delphi is Dungeons and Dragons, which is played by several players at the same time—each one taking a role and trying to avoid whatever disaster is at hand.

Another option of Delphi that clearly falls under the category of entertainment is the ongoing collaborative novel-writing option. People contribute to the novel in progress and watch to see how others add to and change the story.

CompuServe has a whole section devoted to Games and Entertainment, accessible from the main menu by entering "6" when you are prompted for a choice, or by typing "GO GAM." At this point you are given several choices:

COMPUSERVE GAMES PAGE GAM-1
GAMES AND ENTERTAINMENT
1. BOARD GAMES
2. PARLOR GAMES
3. SPORTS GAMES
4. GAMES OF CHANCE
5. ADVENTURE GAMES
6. WAR GAMES/SIMULATIONS
7. SPACE GAMES
8. EDUCATIONAL GAMES
9. FORTUNE TELLING GAMES
10. GAMER'S GAZETTE AND SIGS

A popular choice on CompuServe is Multi-player Casino, which you can enter by typing "GO GAM-1" and then selecting "4" (Games of Chance). Within the Casino, the machine will determine if you have ever been there before. If not, you will be given a new play money account to use in your choice of games. You have at least $1,000 in "cash" to fritter away.

Multi-player Games

Multi-player Social Blackjack is, CompuServe claims, the only game of its kind in the world. You can play against the computer if no other players are around, or you can play with other subscribers. You can elect to be dealer or let someone else deal. If you want to ease into it, you can simply sit quietly and watch the game for a while, psyching out the other players. Players can kibitz one another, but spectators can't take part directly in the talk. If you are a blackjack player, this is a great chance to hone your skills against players from all over the country. Most important, you are all actually playing at the same time just as you would be if you were sitting around a card table in your den. In addition to the fun of the game, you get an opportunity to meet other people on the system.

There are other multi-player games on CompuServe, all of which let you enjoy the fun of game-playing while you're having fun with other people. If you're a musician, you will enjoy the "Orch-90" music special interest group. One of the options in this SIG, "GO HOM-13," is to participate in making music with your computer. Tandy Corporation's Orchestra-90 stereo music synthesizer is the focus of the group's activity. Various applications for the Orchestra-90 are discussed, including sheet music transcription, music theory and recording sessions. The creator of the Orchestra-90 synthesizer is a member of the group and an occasional featured guest at conferences. If you're interested, you can find out all you need to know by joining the SIG.

If listening to music rather than creating it is more to your taste, you might want to call up Joe Ely's bulletin board. "Campfire Nightmares," this country music star's network, was announced on one of his record albums. The board was set up to put fellow fans in touch with each other and the star. The board allows you to call in and leave notes, get on Ely's mailing list, read the itinerary of Texas performers, read a local music column, suggest lyrics, song ideas or do anything else that seems appropriate.

Ely uses computers and electronic synthesizers to produce many of his songs, so the bulletin board is simply an extension of that interest. To use this system, you call (512) 472-6028 and when asked for a user I.D., you type "ELY." You can then look over the system and decide whether you really want to be a fan or not.

This high-tech fan club is an example of one of the creative ways that people can use regional utilities. Campfire Nightmares was established in conjunction with The Electric Pages. You do not have to be a subscriber to The Electric Pages, however, since Ely has paid your dues for this particular section. He has, in effect, set up a local bulletin board without having to do the technical work. Any group with the necessary funds could do the same. The result is that people who call in have a real sense of communication with other fans, the musician and his staff that never existed when you sent in your fan-club dues and got a little card back in the mail.

One thing to keep in mind when you are enjoying the fun on information utilities is that you can share that fun. Just as you play board games with members of your family, you can play computer games with them as well. If you are a trivia buff, CompuServe offers a trivia section with tests to challenge your skills. Although you can play alone, it is fun to play with another person. Your spouse, your kids, your friends will all enjoy testing their skills, and in the process you are sure to share a few good laughs and spend relaxed, happy time together. CompuServe's Trivia section is accessed by typing "GO TMC."

Lois, Tom, Jenny and Bob are all trivia buffs. They were among the first to go out and buy Trivial Pursuit, but one of their favorite ways to spend an evening is by calling into CompuServe and matching their wits against the utility's trivia game. Since they are all experts, they always choose the hardest level of the game, but it is offered for children and novice adult players as well. Once they are on-line, they sometimes take turns answering questions and compare scores. Other times, they combine their expertise to outwit the machine. The first person to answer correctly a Bonus question gets a special reward from the other players. However they decide to play the game, it is always fun. All of them enjoy an evening of good laughs, with good friends, all courtesy of networking.

Charles and his son, on the other hand, enjoy playing war simulation games. Knocking out space-invaders, battleships or whatever threat appears graphically on their screen is a fun way for them to spend time together via electronic networks. Many networks offer games which are similar to video arcade games that parents and children can enjoy together. Whether they take turns trying to outwit the enemy or combine their firepower, Charles reports that these game-playing evenings offer a lot more opportunity for sharing than an evening watching television ever did. Chuck, the son, has even come away on occasion with new respect for his father's quick draw.

Another fun and interesting section of TMC is a group of questionnaires called "So You Think You Know Me!" To find out how well you and your spouse or friend or offspring know each other, each of you answers several questions privately and then the answers are compared. For example, my daughter and I took the quiz together. First the computer asked me several questions about myself, which I answered—questions like "What is your favorite color?" "What is one thing you and your daughter will never do together again?" "What would you do with a day all to yourself?" Then she answered the same questions the way she thought I would answer them. When we had finished the questionnaire, our answers were displayed for comparison. We were able to decide whether or not they were the same, allowing for differences in phrasing and spelling. The computer then told us the results and gave us an idea of how well she knew me. We repeated the process, with different questions, to find out how well I knew her. The whole thing cost less than a movie for one of us; we had some good laughs over some of the answers, and we learned some things about each other as well. Communication through computers need not be a long-distance affair, although it shines in that area. If you can improve communication with people close to you by using the machine, it is indeed valuable.

If you are a programmer, you might be interested to know that the networks are always interested in finding new games. Morris has been programming for a living for years and programming for fun for about as long. A few years ago, he devised a game which simulated a battle at sea. He shared the game with his friends and they enjoyed playing it as much as he did. After some discussion, one of the utilities put the game on-line and now thousands of people can enjoy Morris's creativity.

The Source also offers a large selection of games and other entertainment options, from Astrology to Wumpus Hunt. Games offered appeal to all ages: Hangman, a favorite among the younger set; chess and checkers for older people; blackjack and craps for the gambler; and many other traditional games. The games section also offers learning opportunities for youngsters in the drill section. Spelling, alphabet, addition, division and typing are among the drills that you can use to help your children learn more quickly while having fun.

Some of the game choices offered by The Source include the following:

Adventure	Blackdragon	Crossword Puzzles
Dodgem	Explore	Football
Golf	Life	Mastermind
Othello	Slot Machine	Tic Tac Toe

Fortune-Telling Games

If you feel you need a bit of inside information to help you keep track of things, The Source also offers horoscopes updated daily, biorhythm charts and the I-Ching. An IQ test will either cheer you up or send you running to more educational sections of the utility. The Source Command Guide lists the necessary commands to find your favorite game.

CompuServe also offers astrology and biorhythm charts. You must have a printer to take advantage of the biorhythm chart. CompuServe's astrology chart is not for amateurs. You have to interpret the information yourself, and for those not in the know it looks like so much gibberish:

GEOCENTRIC PLANET POSITIONS
(LONGITUDE,LATITUDE, DECLINATION)
    SUN MERC VENUS MARS JUPIT SATUR URAN
NEPT PLUTO MOON NODE P. F.
    8P35 7P27 22A39 10Q8 24V21 3C53 9G10 5P46
8L29 14V3215C46 1 3V55

This is not the kind of stuff you see in the horoscope section of the paper, where they tell you about tall handsome strangers and to be sure to take care of finances.

Video Games at Home

If you really like video games and enjoy playing them alone or with others, your communicating machine may be just what you need. Coleco Industries, Inc. and a division of AT&T have jointly agreed to bring video games and entertainment software into homes through telephone lines. Coleco is developing a modem that will work with a variety of home computers and game-playing machines. It will sell for less than $100. By using this modem and the transferred software, you won't need the machine for which the software was originally developed.

Atari and Activision have a similar agreement to provide games originally developed for Atari 2600s. The service will be available on different personal computers and will offer other companies' software in addition to Atari and Activision. Users will pay a monthly charge and have many games to choose from. The project was scheduled to begin sometime late in 1984.

Entertainment

There are a lot of ways besides playing games to entertain yourself via electronic networking. Sports, the arts, movies, and literature all fall under the category of entertainment, and electronic networks offer a wealth of choices in all these areas. The Source, for example, offers movie and television reviews. Delphi has a Hollywood gossip column. CompuServe has a sports quiz and a sports special interest group.

There are also several local bulletin boards dedicated to fun of various types. If you're a die-hard limerick fan, you can call up the Limericks BBS in New Brunswick, New Jersey. This board is designed as a place where people who love limericks, trivia and quotations can run amuck to their hearts' content. The phone number is (201) 572-0617.

Dickenson's Movie Guide, in Mission, Kansas, offers an on-line directory of movies playing in the Kansas City Dickenson chain of theaters. Short summaries of movies playing and coming attractions, plus playing time, will be of interest to movie buffs across the nation. Articles on current films and their background are also available on the system. If you want to join the BBS, you can follow the usual password procedure. If you just want to read the movie listings, you can call (913) 432-5544 and enter "Guest" when you are asked for your user ID and "Pass" when you are asked for a password.

If writing short fiction or poetry is your idea of a good time, there are several ways you can participate in "electronic publishing." Electronic publishing is another idea that has not really come into its own yet. Getting your work published by a traditional print publisher is an arduous task. Print is an expensive medium and publishers are circumspect in selecting new authors. Electronic publishing, on the other hand, is relatively inexpensive, and hundreds of people can leave their creative works on-line for others to read and comment on. There are usually no royalties for the author, but if you want to see your work being read, electronic publishing may be the way to go.

Delphi offers an Author's Corner where you can leave your stories or poems for people to read, and where you can set up a conference to discuss your work with others. This discussion can be very helpful to aspiring writers who are working in a vacuum and need to hear how others respond to their work.

Several local bulletin boards have also been established with the aspiring author in mind. Magazine-80, at (603) 924-7920 in New Hampshire, has a section containing a variety of stories, reviews and poetry created by members of the board. David Hughes's Old Colorado City Electronic Cottage, (303) 632-3391, has a section for writers. David especially encourages poets because he feels that the visual quality of the video screen is very sympathetic to poetic creation. The Notebook, in West Palm Beach, Florida, (305) 686-4862, serves as a forum for writers and editors to get together and discuss their interests.

Several BBSs are dedicated to science fiction. Many others offer space for sci-fi discussions and cooperative writing.

Creating art is another way that people enjoy themselves through electronic networks. CompuServe has a special interest group of people interested in electronic and other art. A lot of people are using their personal computers to create graphics and other artistic designs. This SIG helps them share information and discuss their hobby with others. Divided into eight sections, the ARTSIG contains information on general art and technology, articles and essays, programs for creating aesthetic output, art products, art education and other areas of interest. Professionals, amateurs and anyone else interested in art use ARTSIG to see what's going on and to enjoy the companionship of other enthusiasts.

The number of boards is growing constantly; there are as many things that people enjoy doing as there are people. A sampling of local bulletin boards just might help you find the specific kind of entertainment that you are looking for.

Just playing around in various systems and boards is fun, but playing with someone else can be even more fun. And making new friends while you play can be the most fun of all. You may be the only person in Patchinpaw who really gets a kick out of limericks, but through electronic networks you can find lots of other people who share your enthusiasm. It's the ability to leap over distances cheaply at any time of day or night that makes electronic networking so wonderfully useful and enjoyable. And when something can be both useful and enjoyable, that's real fun.

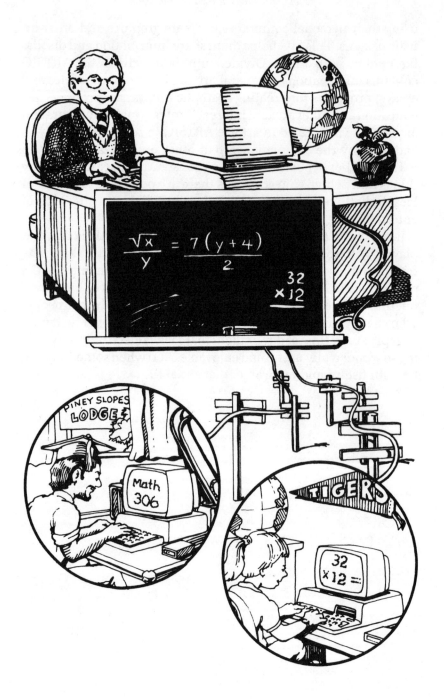

6

Learning at Home or on the Road

Education on the Networks

To communicate is to transfer ideas, feelings, values and information. To communicate is to teach and to learn. Electronic networking—communicating with people of all ages and backgrounds from all over the country—is one of the best and most exciting opportunities for learning that has ever been available to people. Just the simple sharing of jokes, information about printers or software, recommendations of movies and books is educational. It allows us to learn how other people think, what they enjoy, what they know.

To the curious mind—and people who use computers to network are undoubtedly more curious than most—every opportunity to talk with another person is an opportunity to gain more knowledge. As a process, networking encourages curiosity, information-gathering and learning. That is both the value and the fun of the process.

People who use computers to do calculations, extract data and forecast weather are undoubtedly learning things. They are learning facts, finding useful numbers and solving problems. But people who use computers to connect with other people are getting an education.

Despite worldwide communications systems, the evening news and the daily paper, most of us live our lives in fairly small circles. We go to work, we talk to people at the grocery store or the PTA meeting or the singles bar. It is still uncommon for people in Massachusetts to have impromptu conversations with people in Montana. But electronic networking opens up that possibility with incredible ease and simplicity. The result is that we are able to find people who share our interests, and perhaps more significantly, people who are very different from us. That is the way we become truly educated—by learning about different ways that people think, different things that excite people, different ideas that we've never before considered. For these reasons, electronic networking is an inherently educational pursuit.

The educational potential of electronic networking is just beginning to be tapped. Most of us are aware of the growing use of computers in the classroom. Every elementary school you pop into either has computers or is having a Halloween carnival to raise money to buy computers. Programs for teaching everything from typing to advanced trig are selling like hotcakes. Several colleges, including Dallas Baptist College and Carnegie-Mellon, are requiring that freshmen students buy computers as well as textbooks. Regrettably, however, many of these schools feel that what their students need to know is how to program. Computer literacy, to them, means programming and nothing more.

One "educator" who has set up a computer school for children was quoted as saying that every child needs to learn programming because it teaches that "things have to be done sequentially, in order, one thing after another." I shuddered to read that. If children are taught that all you can do with computers is program them and that everything has to go in an orderly straight line, where is the creativity of the future coming from? Children need to know about computers precisely because they are new and fraught with possibilities which can be explored only by people willing to get off that straight path and try something innovative. Children need to be allowed to play with computers, to discover their potential, not just made to march in straight lines. We have military schools to do that.

The bright side of schools' requiring their students to own computers is that networking will almost inevitably follow. Just as it is impossible to imagine a teenager sitting in a room with a telephone for very long without making a call, so these students will find their computer—an excellent communications device—irresistible. Some of the professors will let them turn in assignments on-line. Others will encourage learning about all the capabilities of the machines. Mom and Dad will be hit up for a modem—"I have to have one!" And networks will flourish. Class notes will be shared on-line. Perhaps a good term paper will make the rounds. Friendships will be formed and a new way of meeting people on campus will have been born. Almost every college of any size already has a computer system at work. Students who have access to the campus mainframe are already creating informal networks for communicating with others working on the system. One of the nicest things about networking is that the same process can be done for serious work and just plain fun—both areas in which college students excel.

Computers as Teachers

Computers are big news in education; although many teachers resist using them, the kids love them. There are a lot of things that can be taught well by computers.

Typing is a good example. Nearly everyone needs to know how to type. Although high-level managers traditionally hate to lay hands on keyboards, it is still the most efficient way to use computers. As young business people who are familiar with computers move up in business and industry, this aversion to typing will probably fade.

Taking typing in school, however, seems a waste of time. Almost anything else would be more fun and provide more educational benefit. What most people remember of typing class is the racket: thirty kids banging away at machines, bells ringing, carriages returning—a symphony of discordant sounds. The teacher assigns a few exercises and these are repeated over and over again, "jfjfjf,kdkdkd,lslsls." A skilled educator is hardly needed for that. Basic instruction in how to do a bunch of mindless exercises is all that is required. A computer doesn't mind giving tiresome exercises, makes little noise and has infinite patience.

Well-developed software can also reduce the stress of learning. A package designed to offer helpful advice and supportive correction is a lot easier to deal with than a harried teacher trying to control a large classroom of demanding students.

Teaching on Networks

Significant learning experiences are often the result of an inspired teacher rather than the subject matter being taught. We are so caught up in the teacher's enthusiasm that we develop our own appetite for the subject. A computer can never really take the place of a good teacher, but electronic networking offers the best of both worlds. It combines the speed and efficiency of computers with the presence of another human being—a human being who can ask and respond to questions, stimulate thought and point out fallacies in our thinking.

Electronic network education is in its infancy. What was perhaps the first class taught through a network was offered by David Hughes through The Source in 1981. Called "Electronic English," the class combined traditional English class material with material specifically designed for electronic networking. In Hughes's opinion, electronic networking requires a new form of speech. Writing on a screen is different from writing on paper or speaking to someone face-to-face.

Hughes offered his thirty-three-hour, eleven-week course for college credit under the auspices of Colorado Technical College. The "lecture" portion of the course was conducted at a specific time each week. Students dialed into The Source to participate, completed assignments at their leisure and sent them to the teacher and each other through Sourcemail. The teacher's evaluations of assignments were returned to the students in the same manner. Students from Australia, Alaska, England and the United States participated in that innovative class, which could not have been conducted any other way so inexpensively.

In November 1982, with The Source undergoing some large-scale changes, Hughes's class was discontinued, but he maintained his interest in the possibilities of remote on-line teaching. A more traditional classroom course, another Electronic English class included techniques for communicating electronically. One-third of the class time was spent on network techniques and potentialities. Still later, Hughes offered a mixed class—some of the students in the classroom with the teacher, others on-line. Students in Alaska, Oregon and New Jersey joined those in Colorado to participate in group discussions and what Hughes called his "electure."

His most recent effort at electronic teaching was a completely on-line class held through a variety of media. Some of the students left their papers with a local BBS, others sent theirs through information utilities. Through these pioneering efforts, David Hughes proved the validity of teaching through electronic networks. It worked for his class, and it can work for many others.

Educational Options

CompuServe also offers some options for people interested in education. A section called EDUTECH contains a project designed for people interested in computer-based learning. The introduction to the section, "GO CAL," explains the project:

> "Edutech project is a 7-year-old organization in the business of developing computer aided learning (CAL) systems for private use in the home.
>
> "Edutech Project Tutorials are designed to be used individually without supervision.
>
> "The tutorials are written in Turtle Pilot Language. Turtle Pilot is an easy to learn computer language developed by teachers for teachers.
>
> "The tutorials can be run by selecting the tutorial library page, then indicating your educational level. The available tutorial will then be displayed for your selection. The lessons are friendly, there is no grading, no one looking over your shoulder and you can proceed at your own pace.

"Comments on the courses are encouraged, and may be sent to us via the User Hotline.

"Teachers and nonteachers alike with expertise to share are encouraged to use Turtle Pilot to develop their own tutorials.

"The tutorial library contains a Turtle Pilot programming course for teachers and the curious user. The Turtle Pilot programming language is also available.

"Have fun."

You can create a new course or take one of the courses already offered on the system. Courses range from primary-school level through post-college level.

CompuServe's Educators' SIG also offers information about new possibilities in electronic education. Made up of teachers, parents, students and others interested in education, the group discusses relevant matters and uses the bulletin board to post notices about new educational options. Because the group focuses on education, it provides current information that would not be readily available elsewhere.

New learning opportunities are becoming available every day. The National Education Corporation is offering independent-study courses on its new EdNET system. NEC's mainframe computer in Scranton, Pennsylvania, has been redesigned to accept on-line study. Originally serving as a testing facility for 60,000 home-study participants, the facility now offers more than forty courses on-line. The system also lets students communicate directly with instructors and take tests on their personal computers. Fees range from $700 to $2,200. Many of the courses are technical, including computer literacy, business management and bookkeeping.

Electronic College

A group of entrepreneurs in California have set up what they call the "Electronic University." Headed by Ron Gordon, chairman of TeleLearning Systems and former chief executive editor of Atari, the system will eventually offer classes in hundreds of areas. To become a student at this new university, a person simply buys one of three packages offered by TeleLearning: the Enrollment package, which includes educational software, communications software and enrollment in the school; the Enrollment & Communications package, which includes the items above plus a modem; or the Enrollment & Communications & Literacy package, which includes the previous items plus a computer literacy course. Prices for the packages range from $89.98 to $299.95. Course fees range from $35 to $150 per lesson-hour, depending on the subject and the notoriety of the professor, and cover telephone charges and transmission costs as well as lectures and auxiliary learning aids. Teachers keep regular office hours during which students can communicate directly with them through the electronic network. Counselors are available on-line twenty-four hours a day for questions that may arise. Packages can be ordered directly from Tele-Learning or purchased at retail computer stores.

So far, the Electronic University is available only on IBM PC, Commodore 64 and Apple IIe computers. This machine-specificity is one drawback of the system. A network that offered on-line courses to anyone with any personal computer would be much more appealing to networkers.

A broad spectrum of course choices is offered by the Electronic University. The best news is that the courses include liberal arts, social sciences, pure sciences and other things you would expect to find at a large university. It is not a purely technical school. Courses are being offered through several universities via the Electronic University. Among the accredited schools offering these courses are Edison State College, Ohio University, University of Nebraska, De Anza College, Central New England College, University of Wisconsin and San Diego State College.

The TeleLearning system also offers courses for all age groups. Included in the course offerings is a personal tutor program for students in grades 3 through 6 in math, reading and science. This program is designed to provide individualized help for young students based on their current level of expertise. A tutor, assigned to each child, diagnoses and prescribes learning activities. The courses can be designed to help a student catch up or simply to improve existing skills.

Non-academic courses that relate to children include "How to Discuss Sex with Your Child," "Reading Aloud to Your Child," "Fundamentals of Music," and "How to Take Tests." Courses are also offered to prepare students for taking college entrance examinations on both undergraduate and graduate levels.

Adult course offerings range from personal achievement classes that include art, cooking, music appreciation, assertiveness training, speed reading, astrology and dance, to professional and career development classes that include business math, accounting, stress management, construction and pilot training.

Another interesting method of electronic course-taking is Control Data Corporation's Plato System. Plato was one of the first computer based learning systems in America. Development started in 1962 at the University of Illinois with a grant from Control Data and the National Science Foundation. Since that time, Control Data has supported the further development of the project and become the sole owner and marketer of the system. First used as training courses for managers, computer operators and programmers, the Plato learning system was expanded to offer more than 8,000 course hours in a wide variety of subjects.

Plato was first introduced to the public in 1976 and is currently being used in business, industry, government, academia and vocational and technical educational institutions around the world. Courses for elementary, secondary and college-level students are available and include such subjects as chemistry, reading, mathematics and computer science.

Access to the Plato system can be gained in several ways. You may be taking a Plato course now if you are enrolled in an educational institution since these courses are used in many schools. You can also go to one of CDC's training centers and use their terminals and software to access Plato. Plato software is available for IBM and CDC computers, and you can subscribe directly if you have the required equipment. For further information, contact your local CDC office or call the home office in Minneapolis, Minnesota, (800) 328-1109.

Some of the benefits of on-line university studies are obvious. The best teachers in the country could be made available to a much larger student body than is now possible. Students who cannot afford full-time university studies could participate by working around their schedules and finances. Dormitory, moving and travel expenses would be eliminated. Problems of time, money and accessibility would become less significant.

The drawbacks are minimal in most cases. Although electronic universities may eventually replace traditional seats of learning, it won't happen in the near future. It seems likely that most of the electronic course-takers will be adults rather than recent high school graduates. These adults will want to learn the material, earn the credits and participate in the course while maintaining job and family responsibilities. The flexibility of the system is ideal for people with multiple demands on their time.

Unquestionably, students who go directly from high school to an electronic university will miss out on the social activities of a traditional school. College is characteristically a time when students leave home and begin their lives as independent people. The supportive atmosphere of other students taking the same tentative steps makes for a much smoother transition. Most people's fondest memories of college have little to do with the classes attended, but a lot to do with communicating.

College is a time to try out new ideas, to learn about things your mother never told you. It is a time to stay up all night talking, to sit around the student union talking, to go to movies and then drink coffee, all the while talking. All that talking is necessary for assimilation of ideas and information. And all that talking is still possible with electronic networking. Perhaps the electronic universities would be wise to install electronic student unions. After all, everyone attending has a computer and modem. Even if the universities don't do it, there is no reason for students not to get together and talk things over—classes as well as anything else that comes to mind.

Electronic Grade School

High-powered universities and sophisticated higher learning systems are not the only ones to offer network-based educational opportunities. For example, the Cheyenne Wells, Colorado, school system, boasting a student enrollment (kindergarten through 12th grade) of 230 students, has set up a BBS system for its students and the community at large. The principal took David Hughes's Electronic English course and was sold on the idea of electronic networking as a viable part of the education process. The bulletin board was set up for turning in papers, asking questions and getting quick answers. It is dedicated to student use during school hours and becomes a community bulletin board in the evenings and on weekends.

Students in an elementary school in Michigan are using computers to get to know students in an elementary school in Alaska. The classes exchange information about their members, communities and lifestyles. The result is that children are learning how other people live in very different parts of the country, and they are learning it in a fun way. Just think of how much more fun it would be to talk to a kid in Alaska about glaciers and the Northern Lights than to read about them in a textbook. The general response to textbook information is "What has this got to do with me?" By getting to know people, the information comes to life: "It has to do with me because I have a friend in Alaska who tells me all this neat stuff."

The Plato network has great potential and is being used at all levels of education. Johnston High School, in Austin, Texas, and CDC teamed up to offer computerized tutoring to migrant students. The company donated four computer terminals and the Austin school district is matching that contribution by providing communications software and terminal maintenance. Because migrant students often miss classwork, they need a way to catch up when they are in school. This system was developed to help them keep up with the rest of the class.

Often new technology is more acceptable to children than to adults. We are set in our ways; they have few preconceptions. Talking to people on a computer makes just as much sense to second graders as talking to people on the phone because they learn to do both at about the same time.

Electronic Continuing Education

Educational networking is ideally suited to adult education. Once their prejudices are overcome, adults can benefit from the flexibility of the system. Always the innovator, David Hughes offered an in-service computer literacy course for teachers in Boulder, Colorado. Hughes taught the course from his home in Colorado Springs. All were connected by The Source and by a speaker phone. Hughes talked into his telephone and his voice was heard over the speaker phone in the classroom. This method allowed him to talk and type at the same time, and allowed his students to ask questions as they worked. This "multimodal" technique proved highly satisfactory for teacher and student alike. The teachers came in with no programming or computing experience but left with valuable information on how to use electronic networking for teaching, research, publishing and word processing—and they left no longer afraid of the computer.

Because electronic networking is tailor-made for adult education, there should evolve many different ways that people can learn electronically. Although many of the courses taught now are noncredit, that does not mean that they do not teach. Many adults want to continue learning and care little for additional college credit. The bureaucracies of most colleges and universities make it almost impossible to take a course simply because you are interested in the subject. You must have a degree plan or a major or a goal of some type. The way our institutions of higher learning are set up, just wanting to know about something is unacceptable. Electronic classrooms can end this problem. St. Louis University now has, through The Source, a course on religion that is open to anyone. There is no reason why many such classes could not exist simply to provide opportunities for people to learn without having to register or attend classes.

The possibilities for electronic classrooms, tutoring, practice sessions, expert teaching and many other kinds of education are virtually unlimited. If it can be imagined, it can be done either through a utility, through a local bulletin board, or by one computer networker connecting up with another via phone lines. Although the physical presence of a teacher is obviously different from the teacher's words on a screen, the latter need not be a less valuable experience. We still have a lot of things to learn about teaching and communicating on-line, but these things can be learned. Just considering the possibility of studying with an expert is enough to excite most people. The number of students a teacher can reach is multiplied dramatically as soon as the teacher is no longer limited by time, location or distance from the students.

Many junior colleges must serve broad geographical areas. These were among the first educational institutions to consider electronic classrooms. Because many of their students are older or less affluent, the idea of having flexible hours and non resident students is very appealing. As a result, many schools across the country are busy planning for electronic networks to serve their students.

Some local and regional networks have already been established with an educational focus. The Electric Pages, a subscription service operating out of Austin, Texas, lists education as one of its major interests. The Electric Pages has already established a network for the Texas Association of School Boards that functions as a central newsgathering place for educators and local school boards. Information about legislation, schoolbook hearings, budget changes and anything else that affects local schools is available through this service. Subscribers can call in to contribute or simply be brought up to date. The Electric Pages is also working closely with Austin Community College to provide the technical assistance and networking capability the school needs to offer on-line courses.

If you are interested in learning more about what your peers are doing in your chosen profession, you have several options. For example, the SIGS in CompuServe's Services For Professionals section offer you an opportunity to learn directly from others in your field. Aviators in one part of the country may be experimenting with new materials that aviators in another part of the country have not yet tried. Talking directly with leaders in your field is the fastest way to learn. Rather than travelling hundreds of miles to attend a conference or seminar, a call to CompuServe can put you in touch with those leaders and their most current information and innovations.

Physicians are one group who have learned the value of on-line conferencing. There are at least two medical bulletin boards. Medical science is progressing rapidly, but most doctors don't have the time to read all the medical literature. Therefore, having access to a pool of knowledge is invaluable. The medical forum of CompuServe also provides for direct communication, and the Medical Newsletter has up-to-the-minute information for anyone interested.

In places like Alaska, where distances are extreme and travel is often difficult, the practicality of electronic networks is obvious. Several bulletin boards have been set up to use public school computers when school is not in session. According to Red Boucher in Anchorage, the space between people is narrowing dramatically through the use of these boards. No location that has a computer and phone lines needs to be isolated again.

When people are too busy or too infirm or too independent to attend school, but are also too curious or too intelligent or too stubborn to give up learning, the value of electronic networking is obvious. When you can experience the joy of learning something new or the excitement of finding out something you've always wanted to know or the pleasure of meeting someone interesting, the wonder is that more people don't take advantage of the opportunities just waiting on electronic networks.

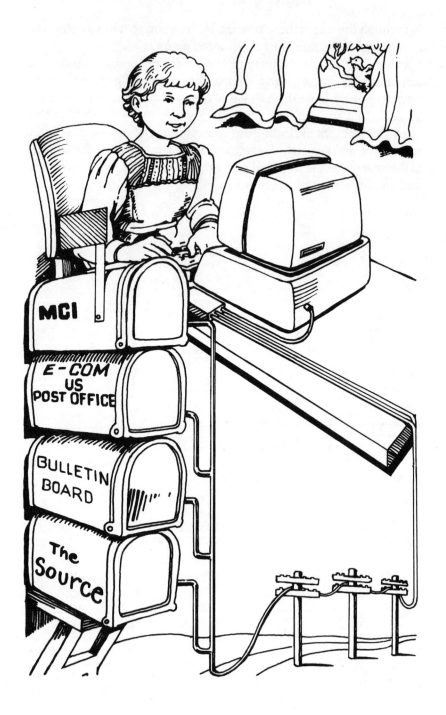

7

Now You Can Live
at the P.O.

Electronic Mail

If there is any area of electronic networking that is familiar to most people, it is electronic mail. Magazines, newspapers, ads and articles are proclaiming the wonders of mail sent electronically. Even the U. S. Post Office has gotten into the act and is offering an electronic mail service of its own.

Electronic mail was first envisioned as a way for business people in large companies to communicate with each other quickly and efficiently. After all, most of them already had computers, and adding mail to their system was relatively simple. Office automation experts have been talking about electronic mail for years, but somehow it was not a bandwagon onto which most businesses wanted to jump. Electronic mail between people in the same company is not as common as one would think. Offices are still awash with memos, and a pile of unread, unanswered correspondence is a traditional feature of the managerial desk.

Electronic mail combines many of the benefits of traditional mail and telephone calls: the ability to plan what you are going to say, revise how you say it and have it all clearly set down that comes with written messages, and the speed and directness of phone calls. Electronic mail is much quicker than traditional mail but avoids the frustrations of busy signals and missed connections that is common with phone calls. With a printer, electronic mail can also be easily translated into the paper form people are often more comfortable with and which can be filed away for future reference.

BBS Mail

People using personal computers knew long before big business that electronic mail is simple, quick and handy. Using the mail function of a local bulletin board is amazingly easy. You call up the bulletin board and select the mail choice from the menu: "E," or "M" or perhaps something else, but always readily identifiable on the main menu. The bulletin board will walk you through the process—(You type the part in quotation marks.)

> WELCOME TO E-MAIL
> WHO DO YOU WANT TO SEND MAIL TO?
> "John Jones"

The system then checks to see whether John Jones is a member of the user community. If he is, it responds:

> TO: JOHN JONES
> FROM: YOU
> SUBJECT?
> "Ballroom Dancing Competition"
> The computer replies,
> TO: JOHN JONES
> FROM: YOU
> SUBJECT: BALLROOM DANCING
> COMPETITION
> JUNE 27, 1984
> YOU MAY BEGIN TYPING IN YOUR MESSAGE

NOW. YOU HAVE UP TO 15 LINES OF TEXT. YOU WILL BE WARNED AT LINE 13.

"Dear John,
"I want to congratulate you on your stellar performance in the ballroom dance contest last Friday evening. Your performance was breathtaking. I hope you will consider entering the upcoming competition at my club, DANCEMANIA, on Saturday, August 15. If you are interested, please let me know and I will forward all the contest rules and particulars.
"Sincerely,
"You"

Since you did not type 13 lines, there was no warning. If you had, however, the board would have interrupted you to say, "WARNING, ONLY TWO MORE LINES LEFT." You could then have cut your letter short and finished up in your allotted space.

Once you have finished your letter, you can edit it, add to it, delete sections, throw it all away or send it on to John's mailbox. If you choose to edit, the board will tell you how. If not, the board sends the letter to John's slot, and the next time John calls the BBS he will find a letter from YOU.

If you wish to communicate with an entire group of users it is a good idea to post your message on a bulletin board. The simplest and most personal way to communicate with a particular person, however, is through electronic mail. Users often make initial contact through public boards and then continue their communication through the more private medium of electronic mail.

The limitations of electronic mail on bulletin boards are obvious. In the first place, not everyone you want to correspond with is going to use your local bulletin board. Unless you spend a great deal of money on long-distance phone calls and use many different boards, your list of possible correspondents is limited. Secondly, because BBSs are small systems they must limit the amount of mail you send and receive. Most systems give you a line limit when you send mail and also allow only so many letters to each user—typically five. When you have five letters in your mail slot, no one else can write to you until you have emptied the slot.

Mail on the Utilities

Once you have discovered the ease and fun of electronic mail on local boards, you will probably want to expand your horizons by using mail services that can reach more people in more places. The Source, CompuServe and Delphi offer mail as well as their other services. There is even some crossover among these utilities; when you are on Delphi you can send mail to subscribers of The Source and CompuServe without having to make another call. The most obvious benefit of using the large utilities is the dramatic increase in the number of people you can reach. By using the utilities' directories you can contact people you don't know but whom you would like to know. The system will give you the address code of any member of the group anywhere in the world—and you are on your way to global connections. If you plan wisely, sending letters through the utilities can be even less expensive than regular mail.

People leaving messages on the bulletin boards of large utilities generally include their mail number so that others can reply. This is one way to find correspondents. If you're looking for people with particular interests, you can also scan the user lists by key words to find those people. If, on the other hand, you want to reach many people, you can compose one letter and send it to many users on the system at the same time.

Each utility has its own method of sending electronic mail, but all are simple to use and have clear instructions. To save time and money, look at your users' manual and plan what you want to say before you call up and begin writing letters. Although all systems are simple to use, the simplicity is masked by the ever-present tendency of computer types to make things sound complicated. When you use CompuServe's electronic mail, for example, you are given a choice of editors. One of the choices is the "FILGE EDITOR." What, you may well ask, is a "filge"? Frankly, I don't know, but it's really easy to use. You may choose to have it explained to you right then by selecting the number which indicates information about the Filge editor. This explanation will be enough to let you rest easy. (It might be a good idea to download or print the instructions for future reference.) Then all you have to do is select "Filge" and start typing your letter. When you are finished, another menu allows you to edit or send it on its way—or toss the whole thing in the electronic trashcan and start over again. It's easy, quick and efficient, even if it is "Filge"!

When you call a local bulletin board, The Source or CompuServe, you can send letters to anyone on that system. When you call Delphi, you can send letters to anyone on Delphi or to anyone on Compu-Serve or The Source whose address code you know. But what if you want to send a letter electronically to someone not using electronic networks?

Electronic Mail in an Envelope

The Source, CompuServe and Delphi all offer access to E-COM, the electronic mail service of the United States Postal System. If you wish, you can set up an account directly with E-COM and send your mail electronically with the assurance that your first-class letter will arrive at its destination right away. The hitch is that to use E-COM directly you have to send at least 200 letters. Even the best of us electronic networkers rarely write 200 letters at a time. The Post Office must also check to be sure your system matches theirs. If you use an information utility to access E-COM, you need no additional equipment and you can send any number of letters you like. You go to the E-COM section of the service, type your letter and the host does the rest. The benefit to you is that the letter arrives in the mailbox of your correspondent without your having to lick the stamp or mail it yourself. There is an additional charge of around $1.50 for E-COM through the utilities, so you'll want to consider cost as well as other factors before jumping in.

If you do send large volumes of mail, a direct E-COM account may be just what you need. The Post Office charges less for E-COM than the utilities do. There is talk of raising the rate, but for now the cost of E-COM is 26 cents for the first page and 5 cents for the second page, two pages maximum. All you do is call in your message and address list to the Post Office computer. The Post Office prints the message and mails it first class to its destination. E-COM lines are open 24 hours a day, seven days a week. If you do a lot of mailing, it would definitely be worth your time to check into E-COM. Contact your local post office for more information.

Another extra-cost option on The Source is to send mail via the Mailgram Message Service. Mailgrams can be sent to anyone in the continental U. S. or Canada, with next-business-day delivery virtually guaranteed. Mailgrams and E-COM are two ways for you to contact people who are not hooked into electronic networks, people who need a piece of paper with your message printed on it.

Computer to Computer Mail

Most electronic mail is between people who use their computers to contact other people with computers. Many young people have found long-distance pen pals through computer networks. Elisabeth in Texas and Martin in New York have never met and probably never will. Both are teenagers who have access to communicating machines. They got to know each other through a BBS and have been carrying on a lively conversation through electronic mail for several months. Both, it turns out, are interested in music and both play in their school bands. The fun of finding out about another person, another part of the country and other school traditions has made their correspondence enriching and enjoyable.

There are many teenagers taking advantage of the networking possibilities of communicating computers. For teenagers, often uncomfortable to begin with, electronic communication is ideal. They can be honest with each other without taking the risks involved in face-to-face meetings. Elisabeth, for example, doesn't have to spend an hour and a half getting ready to talk to Martin on the computer. Martin, in turn, doesn't have to put on a suit and worry about his cowlick to enjoy Elisabeth's company.

Many teenagers participate in networks without revealing their ages, and it gives them a welcome opportunity to be thought of as people rather than kids. Regrettably, many adults tend to discount the opinions and ideas of teenagers simply because they are teenagers. Because one's age, personal appearance, race and sex are not immediately apparent on a computer, people can meet and get to know each other without the prejudices that often occur in personal meetings.

Corresponding with kids on a network can be an educational experience for adults. One of the sysops of a local board is a high school senior, and a brighter, more articulate young man you are not likely to meet. Marge chatted with him several times before learning his age, and by then she was convinced of his intelligence and plain good sense. Marge is a grandmother who, on more than one occasion, has voiced disparaging remarks about young people. It is a delightful surprise when bad old prejudices are washed away by good new friends.

Older people are another prime group of users for electronic mail. Because they often find it difficult or dangerous to get out of the house, being able to communicate electronically is a real boon for them. Ann, a widow who lives alone, finds that electronic mail provides a great way to meet people and keep in touch with them. As with teenagers, people often have prejudices about the elderly. Ann often finds, after much communication, that people are surprised to learn her age—as though someone her age were unable to carry on interesting conversations. Because Ann is limited financially, she is unable to travel and meet new friends. Her computer has provided a new interest in life and access to hundreds of interesting people.

Another benefit of electronic mail is that it can be sent at any time of day or night. You will find that people who use electronic networks tend to be night owls. The networks are busier late into the night than during regular daytime hours. The reasons are simple. People have things they must do during the daytime; most utilities are less expensive at night; and people often enjoy a little companionship in the evenings. In any case, if you wish to send a message at midnight, there is no reason not to send it (something not always true of phone calls). You are also likely to find that one of your correspondents has left you a message as well. Many people send all their electronic mail in the evening and check for replies first thing in the morning.

MCI Mail

Several businesses are concentrating on electronic mail service—for example, MCI, which made a name for itself as an alternative to telephone company long-distance service. MCI Mail is attractive because it is less expensive than many other services and is very speedy. Although the major target of MCI's campaign for users is businesses, individuals can use the service as well.

MCI allows you to send your message directly to another computer or have it translated into printed form. The service can also reproduce logos and trademarks so you can send your message on your own letterhead. When you decide to send a letter through MCI Mail, you choose between sending it direct to another subscriber, sending it through regular mail, having it hand-delivered or having it delivered in four hours—guaranteed.

Signing up with MCI Mail is free; all pricing is message-based. Since there is no charge for connect time, you can spend as much time as you want composing and reading your mail. MCI Mail also offers direct billing while utilities generally do not. If you try to refrain from using credit cards, this can be a big advantage. The price of your message depends on the option you select for delivery. If you are sending computer-to-computer, the cost is only $1 per message. Prices increase to $25 each for letters delivered in four hours. If you send mail often, the savings of MCI Mail can be appreciable. Remember, if you send mail through The Source and CompuServe, you are paying connect-time charges for time spent writing and reading your mail, and both the sender and receiver has to pay the charges. With MCI Mail, only the sender pays.

If you want to send MCI Mail to another computer, both you and the person you are sending to must be subscribers. You simply call the local MCI number, connect as you would to a local bulletin board and leave your message. If you are sending a letter across the country, your correspondent will also call a local number to receive your message. It is possible to register directly with MCI by calling (800) 323-7751. When you are connected, hit "return" twice to indicate a 300-baud modem and enter "REGISTER" when it asks for your user name. The system will prompt you the rest of the way and send you a user ID number. If you prefer to register by phone with a person talking on the other end, call (800) MCI-2255. A packet of information about procedures, rates and such will be sent with your user ID.

Mail Options

In addition to MCI Mail, bulletin boards, E-COM and information utilities, there are several other ways of sending electronic mail. GTE Telenet, Tymnet, General Electric Information Services and Western Union also offer computer-to-computer communications services. Western Union EasyLink service can connect you to computers and Telex terminals around the world. Your messages arrive in writing in just minutes either on Telex terminals or in the printed form of a Western Union Mailgram. As an EasyLink subscriber, you get your own Telex number and can receive messages from anyone else on the worldwide network. News, stock market information and other business-related information are also provided to subscribers. You can sign up on EasyLink at computer stores or by calling (800) 336-3797, Extension 108 (in Virginia, (703) 448-8877, Extension 108).

The electronic mail business is hot right now; new vendors are entering the marketplace at record speed. Software and hardware manufacturers are also jumping on the electronic-mail bandwagon. A user-friendly software package called Master Messenger was written specifically for people who use electronic mail extensively. This package allows the user to write messages off-line for bulletin boards and letters and thereby reduce connect time, phone bills and money spent. You can spend as much time as you want preparing your message, then simply dial into a system and upload it.

Sophisticated modems are especially useful if you plan to do a lot of communicating through your computer. If you buy a smart modem that can answer automatically and are willing to put in a phone line for your computer's exclusive use, you can have your correspondents call you directly and leave messages on your machine. They, like automatic answering machines, collect messages and play them back for you when you're ready to read them. They have something called a buffer—a kind of holding tank that collects the messages. When you're ready to read your messages, you transfer them from the buffer to your disk and then read what has been left for you.

If you aren't ready to install a phone line and leave everything running all the time, you can still get direct messages on your computer. You can connect your automatic answering modem when you leave home and messages can be left then. Of course, people who call on voice phones will be somewhat alarmed when they hear the computer's piercing tone answer the phone. Another option is to let your computer pen pals know when your modem is connected and have them leave messages at those times.

The simplest method of using electronic mail is through one of the mail services, either a specifically mail-oriented system or a bulletin board or utility. These require no hardware or software besides what you already have. Mail services are fast and efficient, and you get your replies quickly. If you want, you can call every morning before breakfast for messages. If you plan to be out of town for several days, your messages will be there waiting for you when you return. It is also worth noting that it is not nearly as aggravating to leave a message on an electronic bulletin board or mail service as on a phone message taker. Most people hate talking to machines—it makes them feel silly. But typing into a message center seems much more natural.

Electronic mail also makes answering mail simpler. When you are faced with a stack of correspondence on your desk, the chore of answering them looks overwhelming. However, a message on your screen that you can answer immediately seems much less intimidating. Usually you don't even have to type in your name or the name and address of the person to whom you are replying—it's all stored in the computer's memory, ready to send your reply right back.

In the age of the telephone, the graceful and time-honored tradition of writing letters has fallen into disuse. A letter-writer is something of a rare bird these days. Still, the letter has charms that the phone call does not. You can pour out your secret poetic soul in letters as you would never dare over the phone. Similarly, you can communicate your absolute disgust in well-chosen words much more clearly in a letter than in conversation. Perhaps the advent of electronic mail will reinvest letter-writing with respectability and people will choose their words more carefully and say precisely what they want to say. After all, any communication works better if you have time to think about what you are saying.

8

Stumping on the Phone Lines

Electronic Politics

George Orwell said, "In our age there is no such thing as 'keeping out of politics.'" In this age, the same could be said of both politics and the technological developments going on about us at breakneck speed. It is only logical that these two consuming passions should inevitably come together.

In 1984, the first presidential election year since personal computers became common in homes and networking became a reality, the usefulness of networking as a political tool is being put to stringent tests. Electronic networks are perfect media for campaigns. In political campaigns, it is often necessary to have staff members spread far and wide. In a presidential campaign there are fifty states to cover; people supporting candidates need to be active in each state and in the counties, cities and towns within them. Still, there must be a central campaign headquarters. There must be consistency among a candidate's statements (ideally, at least) and there must be a way for national campaign headquarters to communicate with regional, state and local campaign headquarters.

In addition, the candidate must keep in touch with headquarters whenever he or she is on the road. Speeches are written at headquarters but delivered far afield. With computer networks, communication can happen efficiently and quickly to make the operation work much more smoothly.

In Anchorage, Alaska, Red Boucher used electronic networks to conduct his campaign for governor. He set up a BBS system to maintain contact with his campaign workers and to enable his staff members to communicate with each other in distant places. He also used The Source to communicate with people in the lower 48 who had an interest in his campaign.

Although his campaign was not successful, Boucher continued to pursue his interests in politics and electronic communications by helping set up bulletin boards in several Alaskan villages. Most public schools these days have at least one computer that can easily be transformed into an after-school public bulletin board. Boucher says, "These bulletin boards have taken the place of old-time public squares where people used to get together to talk and leave messages for each other. With the bulletin boards in the schools, they can call up from out in the country and be a vital part of the community."

These public bulletin boards serve many purposes. They can announce rallies, post public notices and serve as an informal town meeting. In places like Alaska where distances are really important, they have the added benefit of letting people participate who might otherwise be excluded.

David Hughes has used electronic networking widely for political functions. A part of his bulletin board, The Old Colorado City Electronic Cottage, is called "Roger's Bar." In Roger's Bar, people air their opinions on political issues. (A note at the beginning of the board states that this is "where good guys and bad guys shoot it out over freedom of speech. You figger out which is which.") In a recent county commissioner election, David's bulletin board profiled several candidates and their positions. Three of the candidates chosen by the bulletin board were elected. The board also generated enough public support to defeat a proposed city housing-occupancy law.

Another use that Hughes has found for networking involves a small business association of which he is a member of the board of directors. Because board members meet regularly with the city council to promote economic development in the area, they are often called upon to make presentations to the council. When they are too busy to hold regular meetings of their own, they often "meet" electronically to decide on their position before they are called upon to speak to the council. Sometimes they meet silently at the council session; they pass Hughes's small TRS-100 computer back and forth, each member entering his or her ideas, to reach a consensus before their turn comes up on the agenda.

Making Your Views Known

There are ample opportunities on electronic networks for people to air their political views. The next step—using the networks to make opinions heard in places of power—will be a quantum jump in the history of grassroots politics. One young man is now travelling the country tapping into bulletin boards and propounding his political beliefs. He is attempting to convince people that his stance against nuclear power is both right and practical, and people seem to be responding. As he travels about, his notices on boards stimulate conversation and comments and get the ball rolling for further discussion.

CompuServe, The Source and Delphi also offer politically oriented bulletin boards and conference options. In the 1984 election year, CompuServe added Democrat and Republican SIGs to their offering. CompuServe's SIGS have regularly scheduled conferences on politics, with visiting politicians and experts to offer their perspectives to the group. Senator Howard Baker of Illinois has even consented to do print advertisements (without compensation) for The Source because he is convinced of its helpfulness in both his private and public communications.

A state senator in Michigan got the idea for a political forum bulletin board and found Gordon Williams to act as sysop. As a result, the senator stays aware of his constituents' concerns, knows what they want him to do for them and is able to respond quickly to their questions and requests. The result is a politician with a genuine knowledge of his constituency and no excuse for ignoring their problems.

Barbara Marx Hubbard, an independent vice-presidential candidate in 1984, designed her campaign as a true grassroots effort. She required all her town groups to set up electronic networks to which every citizen could have access. The towns, in turn, communicated with county and state organizations and built pyramid-style to the national level.

Computer Lobbyists

Aside from getting elected, one of the best ways of influencing legislation is through lobbying. Electronic networks are perfect lobbying tools. Because members of any group are bound to be somewhat scattered geographically, electronic networks are very efficient in bringing interested parties together. Many regional utilities serve as collection points for data lobbyists needing to press their causes.

The Electric Pages is located in Austin, the capital of Texas. Because it is the seat of the legislature, it is also a focal point for most of the state's lobbying activities. The lobbyists have to be in Austin to present their cases to the legislators. The people who have a vested interest in the results, however, may be in Austin or hundreds of miles away in Amarillo or Laredo or Texarkana. Communication must be maintained between the lobbyist and the people who are paying him or her to represent their interests. This communication is often conducted via regional networks or utilities.

The Texas Association of School Boards uses The Electric Pages to stay informed on issues relating to education. When the legislature is in session, The Electric Pages provides TASB a bill-tracking system that allows subscribers to receive timely information on education bills in the house and senate.

Almost every profession or trade has a union, association or organization with an interest in legislation that might affect its members. Headquarters of these organizations are typically in state or national capitals, or both, and their effectiveness often hinges on the quality of communication between members and their representatives. TASB and other associations have learned that there are many benefits in establishing electronic networks. Not only can the local members communicate their views and needs to state headquarters, but also they can communicate among themselves. A school board in Houston can tell a school board in Tyler how they solved a local problem, and the information can help save time by avoiding false starts. Most school boards face similar problems and political situations. Being able to share information and expertise helps every member of the network do his or her job better.

According to Orbry Holden, executive director of TASB, "Information is the key. Being able to access information quickly is important to all of us. What we want to do is provide school districts the capability to ask for and acquire information as they need it. The Electric Pages provides a communications vehicle that doesn't depend on someone else being on the other end of the phone at a certain time. We need a direct link between school districts and TASB on legal questions; we need the ability to do surveys so we can question the districts on certain issues and get their responses quickly. An electronic network provides these capabilities."

Polling

Holden's comments point to another political use of networks; the ability to conduct polls electronically. Computers have been used for polling for several years, but primarily for tabulating results. Few polls have actually been conducted electronically. Being able to poll their members quickly and easily will encourage groups to use networks more and more often.

Networks are being set up in the government itself because they are proving themselves better for communication than either paper or phone. The busier people are, the more difficult it is to catch them on the phone or get them to sit down and write a letter. With networks, time of day is not a consideration and the process of communicating one's thoughts goes much faster than sifting through stacks of paper.

Direct Mail

Electronic mail is ideal for political uses for the same reasons. Most politicians conduct at least one direct-mail campaign per election. Most citizens' groups also produce flyers, letters and position papers to support their candidates. Any of these can be quickly written and disseminated by electronic mail. The sender can use both electronic and paper delivery and canvass a large area in a very short time. Because electronic utilities allow you to search the user base for the particular people you want to reach, your campaign is more likely to reach its targets. On the other hand, if you have a large geographical area to cover, the mail services allow you to send the same piece of mail to hundreds of people more easily than by regular mail. That old staple of political campaigns—the envelope stuffer—may soon be a thing of the past. Once the candidates have been elected, they may also choose to keep in touch with supporters and hear constituents' concerns through electronic mail. Some utilities provide services that enable you to write directly to your congressman or senator.

Broad-based Communications

Communication in government is sometimes so bogged down in protocol, red tape and formality as to be nonexistent. A networking capability offers politicians an opportunity to communicate and perhaps even accomplish some of their goals quickly. A new network designed to increase the efficiency of the federal government has been established to link up some of the most influential officials in Washington. Called Executive DataLink, this electronic mail system allows the White House and other governmental agencies to send in minutes messages that used to take days. It connects agency officials and White House staff members via a data center maintained by CompuServe.

Networks are also being used to discuss the pros and cons of nuclear disarmament. Congressman Edward Markey (D-Mass.), an advocate of arms control and a leader of the nuclear weapons freeze movement in Congress, has opened a PARTI conference on The Source both to discuss his views and to hear the views of others. Source users can read Markey's comments and leave their own in response, rebuttal or agreement. The first two position papers Markey left in the conference were entitled, *The U.S.-Soviet Nuclear Balance* and *The Nuclear Freeze: Can It Be For Real?*. Besides stating his position, Markey also asked members of the group five questions, such as "Who do you think is ahead in nuclear weapons—the United States or the Soviet Union?" and "Do you think it makes any difference at this point who is ahead?" Once Congressman Markey has finished making his contribution, the conference can continue without him; proceedings are recorded for any Source user to read.

According to Ron Klain, Congressman Markey's legislative assistant, the congressman is interested in stimulating discussion and hearing in-depth, thoughtful responses from people he would not have known otherwise. Klain points out that most media, TV and radio in particular, don't allow time to give a detailed viewpoint. Electronic networks, however, allow conferees as much time and space as they need. The networks also allow many more people to participate.

Any political effort requires keeping up with current events. The wealth of news services available on-line is enough in itself to justify a politically active person's subscription to a utility. *The Washington Post, The New York Times, The Wall Street Journal* and many other daily papers are available. With the ability to search the databases for topics that interest you, you can save hours in news gathering alone.

For some time now computers have been used to tabulate votes, analyze polls and project winners for television networks. Now computers make possible active political participation by anyone with a computer and modem. They offer a way for politicians to learn the feelings, needs and concerns of their constituents. People have been banding together for years to influence the political process, but before now it had to be primarily a physical banding. People had to hold meetings that were not always convenient to attend, plan for the next meeting, play telephone tag in arranging strategy and spend hours typing and stuffing envelopes. All this was designed simply to make their representatives aware of their opinions. This time can be drastically reduced or at least put to more fruitful uses through electronic networking. Besides saving time and making direct connections, electronic networking can establish a broader political base because people who cannot or will not attend meetings can still contribute their thoughts and ideas.

If networks become widely available and accessible through school computers or other public facilities, many people who have otherwise felt disenfranchised can have a voice in the political process. The disabled, the housebound, the elderly and the physically isolated can call into a network and contribute without ever having to be physically present at a caucus or rally.

9

Finding Friends and Maybe Lovers
Personal Relationships On-Line

If there is one time we most often wish for a magic carpet, it is when we seek romance. "Fly me to my perfect mate!" we would willingly command. Electronic networking cannot guarantee that you will find your dream mate, but it can offer you a way to meet others looking for companionship.

In the early stages of electronic networking, the goals were twofold. First, networks were an extremely efficient form of business communication. Second, the people who spent all their time in front of terminals got rather lonely after a while, so making friends became another primary use. As the medium grew, people became fascinated with the possibilities of electronic communication and began developing ways to meet each other.

All the services mentioned in previous chapters touch on ways people meet. A by-product of any exchange—whether it be discussions of technology or game-playing—is the possibility of developing friendships.

From talking to people over a network you get a sense of what they are like, how they think, what they enjoy and whether you would like to know them better. Mike, a regular participant on local boards, says, "This whole business of 'chatting' on-line to someone is very spooky. It's almost like talking directly to another person's mind. You can get intimate very quickly with someone without ever seeing them face to face."

Mike's comment points out one of the major benefits of electronic networking in making friends: there's no risk involved. From the beginning, you are anonymous. You have a password but no face, no physique, no personal statistics to identify you. You can be as frank as you wish without fear of embarrassment.

Making Friends

People who are shy about meeting people find electronic networking the perfect medium for making new friends. You can find out a lot about another person without having to endure the jittery nerves or tumbling stomach that are involved in first-time face-to-face meetings.

Many people make friends through electronic networking and keep in close contact with them without ever meeting in person. James is an avid networker. He participates in The Source as well as local bulletin boards around the country. When he began networking, he was interested in finding people who shared his passion for computers as a hobby. He called up several bulletin boards in various parts of the country and made quite a few contacts. He also subscribed to The Source and began to make friends in different parts of the country. James says, "I have established friends with whom I communicate regularly and yet have never met face-to-face."

Despite the abundance of singles bars and singles clubs, there is still a need for new ways to meet people. Here is an example of how electronic networking worked for Hal:

"A few years ago, I worked at a local university in the computer lab. I soon found out that there were many young women using the system to meet guys on campus. They used 'handles' instead of real names, but as they got to know you, they played a game of giving little clues as to where they worked. I talked on-line to one girl, Becky, and found that we had many mutual interests. We conversed for several weeks, sometimes staying long after work hours. One night the conversation got sexual. We got bolder over the next few nights and I decided to piece together the clues she had given and get a look at her. I found her two days later on the other side of the campus. (I went into her office and pretended to be lost. She didn't know me.) After seeing her, I decided to suggest a meeting. I invited her to my place and she agreed. The first time I met Becky in person, I felt like I knew everything about her. She felt the same way. I'll leave the rest to your imagination."

Hal met Becky through direct communication on a local area network. The same kind of thing happens on local bulletin boards all the time. People get involved in ongoing conversations and decide they are interested enough in each other to meet in person.

Electronic Matchmaking

Once the interest in finding friends or dates or lovers was recognized, a whole new approach sprang up. In many areas, there are bulletin boards specifically designed for matchmaking. The software, designed for Apple computers, can be purchased and put up on an existing board, or it can be a board by itself. The primary purpose of these boards is to help you meet new people, establish contact with others, and eventually perhaps, make face to face contact.

Known as Dial-Your-Match and often listed as DYM#____ on bulletin board listings, the matching services make their intentions clear from the beginning. Dial-Your-Match is a trademark of and is copyrighted by Matchmaker Enterprises. A typical introduction to the system says:

"This D-Y-M is for your fun and pleasure. Ours is a straight-oriented board with personal electronic mail and a unique matching service.

"Before you can d-y-m, you must answer a questionnaire giving the computer information about yourself. The computer will then be able to match you to other compatible callers.

"WARNING!!! All information in the following questionnaire may be released to anyone calling this system.

"Remember! None of your personal information is confidential and you must complete the questionnaire to be allowed on this system.

"Do you want to continue?"

If you decide to enter the "date-a-base," the system proceeds with the questionnaire. For each question, you are given a choice of answers; for example, one question might ask "How would you describe your lifestyle?" The choices might be: "A) I live in the fast lane, B) I live life day by day, or C) I have carefully planned my life." Once you have finished the questionnaire, you have other choices; however, your questionnaire remains on file for other people to peruse and ponder to decide whether they want to get to know you. One of the choices—usually the first—is to ask the system to find you a match. After comparing your answers with those of others, it gives you the name and address code of people who have answers close to yours. It also gives you a percentage of similarities—so you can talk first to Mr. 80% Right, then work your way down to Mr. 50% Right. You can look at your match's questionnaire to find out more about him or her and then choose to send that person some mail. Depending on the person sending it, this mail can range from "Hello, we have some things in common" to "My address is 123 Maple, stop by at 8."

The main problem with DYM boards is that most of the people who use them are male. A woman is likely to find 150 matches, while a man may find only three. In any case, the boards are extremely popular, and getting through the busy signal is a real challenge.

In addition to regular boards and matchmaker boards, there are other boards with explicitly sexual purposes. Some are in the nature of electronic heavy breathing; others allow people to talk in a non-threatening way about their sexual fantasies. Still other boards cater to members of various subgroups: there are gay boards and teen boards.

CB Good Buddies

One of the most widely publicized events to come out of the large utilities was the case of a couple who met and later married via electronic networking. George and Debbie Stickles met when he, from his apartment in Texas, and she, from her home in Arizona, signed onto CompuServe's CB channel. After preliminary chatting, with other people on the line, George and Debbie decided they were interested enough in each other to continue their conversation on a private channel. That first conversation lasted for eight hours.

A week and a half and several conversations later, they talked for the first time on the telephone. Four months after George and Debbie met via CompuServe's CB, they were married—via CompuServe's CB. On Valentine's Day the happy couple, decked out in their wedding finery, sat before a terminal decorated with white doves. A minister read the vows while his assistant typed them into another machine. A third terminal was "played" by an organist who typed an original rendition of the wedding march: "Dum Dum De Dum." The bridesmaid was in New York, the bride's parents in Arizona, her sister in California—all participating in the service via their home computers. Specially invited guests signed onto the closed channel and there were even a few sniffs from the witnesses. When the ceremony was finished (with a rousing "KISS"), showers of exclamation points, commas, and asterisks fell upon the new bride and groom.

"Mr. & Mrs. Mike," as they are known on CB now are the proud parents of a "CB baby" and keep in touch with friends they have made on the system.

CB is unique in its ability to bring people together electronically. Terry Biener keeps up with what is going on in CB society and writes a regular column on the system. Terry's own story is indicative of the ways CB helps people make friends.

"I'd been a schoolteacher for several years but quit teaching to stay home with my baby. As with many young mothers, I enjoyed being with the baby, but after a while I got bored. I missed the opportunity to converse with individuals in the business world and other professionals. I needed mental stimulation and longed for intelligent and interesting conversation.

"Almost immediately I became addicted. My mind became active again. My vocabulary improved. CB is a social event. It's similar to going to a party. People meet and become acquainted. It's a totally different social interaction than simply leaving messages on a bulletin board. The talk is spontaneous and direct. In some ways it's like writing to your diary and having someone answer you.

"I've met more than 300 people in person that I first met on CB and a lot more than that on-line. There's a feeling of camaraderie and closeness that I just have never experienced anywhere else. People have parties and any CBer in the area will come. It's sort of like a high school reunion. It takes a little while to feel comfortable, but then you realize you're in the midst of a bunch of old friends.

"After the initial shock of face-to-face meetings, there is a feeling of great warmth. People offer other CBers a place to stay when they are visiting. All sorts of conversations go on all the time. People meet on an open channel and then may go to a private mode to talk. A lot of people come to CB first when they subscribe to CompuServe. It's a way to break the ice and see what the possibilities of the system are. A lot of people think of CompuServe as information, but CBers think of it as a place to make friends."

Terry soon saw a need for a society column to help CBers keep up with what was going on. She made a proposal to CompuServe and they agreed. Her column, "CB Society—Cupcake's Column," is a wealth of information about what's going on with the people who use CB. Terry's handle is "Cupcake," and her column includes interviews, introductions of new members, party reviews, youth news and gossip. Although everyone uses handles, there is no great shield of anonymity. People keep up with one another's careers and social lives as if they were all living in a small town, the only difference being that members of this community may live thousands of miles apart.

To give you a taste of the possibilities for making friends and lovers on CB, here are some excerpts from Cupcake's Chatter:

****

"LOVE AT FIRST BYTE

"It was only Sunlight's second day on CompuServe when she met Dustin on CB. One month later, wedding plans were in the future for them, including a total relocation for her and her two children from San Francisco to Pittsburgh.

"During that time span, CB talks, phone calls, photograph exchanges and a five-day visit led to an emotional bond that the couple felt could last forever.

"Sunlight, previously a kindergarten teacher, has been managing a casino rental company used by fund-raising organizations. Dustin is a psychiatrist and practices at a state hospital in Pennsylvania.

"Sunlight is planning on her move from California within the next two months."

****

"CB BREEDS ALL KINDS OF RELATIONSHIPS
"CompuServe has certainly affected the life of Gold Unicorn, formerly known on CB as Feline in L.A.

"One evening on CB she met Red Baron, from Rhode Island. They spoke on their terminals and over the phone, rapidly becoming good friends. Red Baron had been planning a move, possibly to California. Gold Unicorn was planning to move from Los Angeles to Berkeley, to attend college there. After three weeks, Red Baron moved to Berkeley to share an apartment with Gold Unicorn. They now live together platonically as best friends. She majors in psychology and he is a salesman in a paint store, planning to attend the University next year to study computer science.

"Recently, on CB, Gold Unicorn met Inspector, a quality assurance engineer from San Jose. After a CB talk and a phone call, Inspector drove 50 miles to the roommates' apartment in Berkeley. He and Gold Unicorn started dating and have fallen in love."

****

"ELECTRONIC ENGAGEMENT
"Love has struck yet another CB couple: Cosi, of Columbus, Ohio, and Sagittarian of Oakland, CA. The two have CBed together, spoken on the phone, exchanged pictures, and now they have exchanged engagement rings via U. S. Mail. They have not, however, met in person yet.

"Cosi, whose handle stands for Columbus Ohio Scientific Institute, works as a volunteer at the museum. In the near future she plans to move to California to be with Sagittarian and to attend college.

"Sagittarian is a salesman for a chimney cleaning company. He describes Cosi as, 'the most wonderful, most beautiful girl in the U.S., who has everything in common with me!'"

****

"W. WANDA WILL WED WIZARD

"After meeting on CB in October, which led to many talks on CB and phone calls, W. Wanda and Wizard decided to be together. In March, Wanda moved from Minnesota to Miami to be with Wizard. Now, after months of knowing each other in person, they have decided to get married.

"The couple is still in awe of the way they met, and say that they could not be happier or more in love. Their exact words were, 'Thank God for CB!'"

****

"IT'S A GIRL ! ! !

"Judy and Tommy Thomas, otherwise known as HB and Desperado, proudly announce the birth of their daughter, Kristen Leia Thomas.

"Kristin is the first baby to be born to a couple who met on CompuServe's Simulated CB system, and later married. Our first CB baby was born on June 18, 1983, in Columbus, Ohio, weighed 8 lbs., 5 oz, and was 21 inches long.

"HB and Desperado may be congratulated through EMAIL."

The number of couples who have met on the CB channel and eventually married is hard to guess. The number of people who have met and established relationships through the thousands of other networks in the country is even harder to imagine.

CompuSex

On the other hand, maybe you aren't looking for love and marriage and CB babies and all that stuff. Maybe what you are looking for is a passionate affair that bursts upon the scene like the Fourth of July and sweetly fades away like spent fireworks in the wind.

Maybe what you are looking for is "CompuSex."

A phenomenon not sanctioned by Cupcake, CompuServe or the official CB operations, CompuSex, has sprung up in spite of the fact that it is discouraged by the service. People meet on open channels and then adjourn to the private /TALK option and proceed to describe in as much detail as they like what they might be doing if in fact they were lovers and not 900 miles apart. Because the people themselves are actually invisible, they can indulge their fantasies without having to worry about guilt, birth control or commitments.

Strangely enough, however, most of the CompuSex goes on between people who are fond of each other and have chatted for some time before the sex begins. Sure, there are Cruisers who make a habit of one-night stands and quickie relationships, but more common are the people who meet time and time again to share their secret love life.

The same kind of explicitly sexual talk goes on all the time on local bulletin boards, but time necessarily elapses between a message and a reply. On CB the reply is instantaneous and conversations can quickly become hot and heavy—all depending on your tastes, of course.

Special Friends

CB has proved to be a special place for a lot of people. Because physical appearance, age and body language are not readily apparent, people who would otherwise find it difficult to make friends find it easy on CB. Another excerpt from Cupcake's Chatter shows why:

****

"A TOUCHING REPLY

"In a recent interview with C. Y. Borg, he answered the question, 'How has CB affected your life?' His reply was so moving, I have chosen to print it here for all to read. Here is what he said:

" 'CB has had a dramatic effect on my life from the first time I got on. I was channel-hopping and made contact with a lady who wished to chat. We talked and I discovered that she was in her mid-twenties, from New York, single and interested in meeting men on CB. I described myself as college-educated, 28, single, a computer programmer who owns his own firm, from Indianapolis and owning seven computers. Impressed, she simply asked, "Looks?" I stopped dead in my tracks. I suddenly realized that there was something about me that everyone I met knew about me, but that she didn't! I am confined to a wheelchair by a form of Muscular Dystrophy. All my life I have been trying to get people to treat me like any other person. I suddenly realized that CB was the perfect opportunity to make friends and meet people without the image of me in my chair blocking the way.

" 'Although my handicap does not leave me disfigured, in my panic I never did answer her. I continued to talk computers and then broke off. Later I realized that I had succeeded in my lifelong quest to free myself of my chair and I didn't really like it. I don't want to deny my handicap because it is such an integral part of my life, who I am, what I feel, my outlook on life. But I know from a lifetime of experience that it can impede the formation of relationships. I need to be open and honest, yet I will not tell of my handicap in search for sympathy. I tell my CB friends about it only if it is pertinent to the conversation. Ask me what's new or about my computers and you might never know about my handicap. CB gives me the option of discussing it or not, but I won't pretend I'm something I'm not!

" 'CB proves I'm as human as any of you. All I ask is to be loved like a human with all my differences and faults intact—not hidden behind a mask.' "

CB is not the only network that has proven helpful to people with handicaps. Milton is a retired air traffic controller and ship's radio operator. He has spent a lifetime communicating with people both professionally and privately. After retirement, Milton was stricken with a neuromuscular disease which makes his speech unintelligible. After months of feeling frustrated and helpless, Milton purchased a home computer. He now uses a voice synthesizer to communicate with people in person, and his keyboard to communicate on networks. It has truly given him a new lease on life.

There is a discussion group within the NIPSIG area dedicated to people with handicaps. "Disability Dialogue" meets every Friday night at 9:30 EST. They discuss emotional problems caused by disabilities and other topics of interest. People who are disabled and people who are interested and have ideas to share are welcome to join the group. A physician has volunteered to answer questions as needed.

Ladies' Aid

One of the problems male networkers face when looking for relationships is that most of the people who network are men. Estimates are that on most boards the population is upwards of 70% male. To encourage women to participate, several local boards have set up special boards for women. Among these is a "Girl Talk" board where women can talk with each other about anything they choose. After signing onto the main board, a woman leaves her name and number with the sysop. He may then call and verify that she is indeed female before allowing her access to the board.

Another kind of board requires a similar process. Both men and women are allowed on these boards, but all men must be recommended by women. When a woman gains access to the board, she is allowed to recommend three men to participate. If she drops out, the men she has recommended are locked out of that board.

This second kind of board is designed as a way for men and women to meet. One of the sysops explains, "We made it a restricted-access board because the problem most computer bulletin boards like this one have is that all of their callers are male. This creates a problem when you have 200 men and only 5 women. With a restricted-access dating board we have a way of controlling the ratio and hopefully of attracting more female callers."

Other general boards have "Want Ads" or "Personal Columns"— space reserved for people to announce that they are looking for friends. These postings are similar to ones you find in other media. A typical ad reads:

"My name is Tom. I am 6'2, 180 lbs, black hair, green eyes, athletic build and pretty good looking. Emotionally, I am very romantic—as much as the other person allows me to be. I really enjoy kissing and whatever follows. I'm a computer information systems major and Catholic. I sail, scuba, swim and like outdoor sports. I'd like to meet some people and chat or whatever! Leave me mail under _____."

In response to this ad, a woman can send Tom a note through electronic mail and thus form a new relationship.

Talk about Relationships

Not only can you find friends and lovers through electronic networking, you can also try to figure out what all this love stuff is about in the first place.

A weekly on-line conference on CompuServe deals with love and friendship. Conducted by Dr. Del Dobyns, the discussion is informal and the process something like an encounter group focusing on relationships. Generally, Dr. Dobyns presents material for discussion and then members of the group talk about their reactions and opinions. Discussions have lasted as long as six hours. Dr. Dobyns says that one of his purposes in starting the group was to see what kind of discussion could evolve on electronic networks. "Surprisingly, it is quite in-depth. Being able to carry on a real-time dialogue with people all across the country is in a way like the old-time notion of sitting on the front porch and interacting with the parade of life on Main Street in front of you. It is just a very exciting, meaningful, stimulating, provocative kind of activity."

Dr. Dobyns is a teacher at Spokane Falls Community College. The group meets on Monday nights at NIPSIG on CompuServe. NIPSIG is the National Issues and People Special Interest Group. Designed as a forum for the free exchange of feelings and thoughts, this SIG is broad in scope and decidedly a people-oriented place. Regularly scheduled conferences deal with human relations, handicap issues, women's concerns, politics and sex-related issues.

If you decide to join the group, you can indicate your own special interests and get in touch with people who share them.

CompuServe also offers transcripts of panel discussions, articles and questions and answers dealing with human sexuality. GO HSX will give you access to this wealth of information.

* *

HUMAN SEXUALITY
1. SPECIAL FEATURES
2. ON-LINE TRANSCRIPTS
3. ANSWERING YOUR QUESTIONS
4. IDEA: TEENS ADVISE TEENS
5. FORUM: RELATIONSHIPS
6. NEWS HIGHLIGHTS
7. CHAT WITH US —NOTES
8. HOTLINE: YOUR MESSAGES?

Whether you want to make a friend, find a lover or mate, or simply discuss the endlessly fascinating subject of human relationships, electronic networking is the place to be.

10

All This and Money Too?
Taking Care of Business

Much has been written about the uses of computers in business, and indeed their primary functions have always been in business contexts. Nothing can process information, do complicated computations and rearrange data as quickly and efficiently as a computer. But what about computer networks? They, too, have been widely discussed as business tools, but their real value has been more slowly recognized.

Every business relies heavily on communication to get its work done. People have to communicate with each other within a company; they have to communicate with prospective and actual customers and clients; they have to communicate with strangers and people they know. Even though more and more businesses, both large and small, are relying on computers to do their bookkeeping, payroll and financial planning, most still use reams of paper for communication: paper for memos between offices, paper for letters to clients, paper for marketing campaigns, paper to keep track of missed phone calls.

There has been a lot of talk about paperless offices and automated offices, but the talk far outstrips the reality, particularly in the area of communication. The reason is that business people, like people in general, are leery of computers; they feel computers are somehow threatening, and they don't know how to use computers as communications devices. The diversity and confusion of technology are also factors in the hesitancy of some businesses to leap into electronic networking.

Local Area Networks

A large industry has grown up around what are called LANS, local area networks. A LAN is a network designed for a particular group of people—generally a business entity. When a company decides to bring electronic networking onboard, it generally must acquire a local area network, and the choices are not simple. Because our interest here is primarily the networker who operates from his or her individual machine, I don't intend to go into much detail about LANs, but it is a commonly thrown-around term and one you may run into.

Usually a LAN provides a network among offices in a geographically limited area—such as an office building, a college campus or a small community. LANs directly connect all the computers and terminals in the network, usually by some sort of cable, radio transmitter or fiber-optics device. Just deciding what sort of connector you need is a difficult task. In addition, each computer within the system must be able to work with all others, so the problem of compatibility becomes major when choosing a LAN to work with existing machines.

The benefits of local area networks, however, are manifold. Because the network is always in place and ready to work, there is no problem of calling into a foreign system or paying connect charges or needing to do something the network does not provide. Electronic messages and mail can fly from one part of the business to another whether both people are at their desks or not, and since the connections are direct, there is no messing with modems or telephones. Sally can leave a message on Jane's computer for Jane to pick up whenever it is convenient. Bob can call into the network from out of town to pick up important messages he might otherwise have missed while he was away. Jane and John can have an impromptu meeting on their computers and make quick decisions without having to leave their offices.

Any private network that connects people within a limited area could be considered a local area network. Many universities have local area networks that connect the various parts of the campus. A lot of time, energy and wasted steps can be saved by having the ability to contact someone immediately—whether they are there or not.

Networks for Business

What about people who have to take care of business but don't work for a company with a local area network? Networking is still often the answer. Because there are already many networks and because new networks can easily be established, taking care of business electronically is a snap.

Drive Your Computer to Work

One of the phenomena that observers of the burgeoning computer age have been quick to point out is that with the capabilities of the machinery, people need not always be physically present at their place of employment. Several companies are operating pilot projects whereby some employees are doing their work at home and sending it to the office via some kind of network. Data entry clerks, for example, can enter data at home as well as they can at work, and the field is thereby opened up to people who might not otherwise be able to work. Mothers with young children they choose not to leave can still get a day's work done by working during naptime, while the children play or in the evenings. If the material is not very time-sensitive, there is no reason it must be entered at 9 a.m. rather than 9 p.m. The work-at-home option also allows physically handicapped people to be self-sustaining, productive employees without having to cope with architectural and emotional barriers that might interfere with travelling to work.

Blue Cross/Blue Shield in Washington D.C. has initiated a Cottage Keying Program which allows ten employees to do their work at home via a network. These ten people are among 10,000 who are trying out this new way of working at approximately 250 companies across the country. Control Data Corporation in Minneapolis has an Alternate Worksite Program in which nearly 100 employees commute via computer on either part-time or full-time bases. New York Telephone, Walgreens, American Express and McDonald's all have programs which they intend to expand over the next few years. The Center of Futures Research at the University of Southern California predicts that by 1990 approximately 10 million people will be working at home rather than commuting to offices.

Many executives find that working at home is more productive and satisfying than working at the office. Without the interruptions of phone calls, meetings and social chats around the coffee pot, work can go more quickly and still leave time for other pursuits. A combination of work at home and work at the office is often best for people whose job requires both creativity and interaction with others. Every office worker in the country has heard the words, "I'm going home so I can get some work done!" Now work can be done at home and transferred to the office automatically so that it is there for further polishing and discussion at the appropriate time.

Some observers have predicted that with the development of networking, more and more people will work out of their "electronic cottages." Because of the sophistication of the technology, physical location is no longer the constraint it once was. It is easier to transmit information electronically than it is to hop in a car and drive across town. And with the networking possibilities that allow actual conversations, points can be argued, compromises made and decisions agreed on without the necessity of personal meetings.

Office at Home—Do Business with the World

Aside from the millions of people who use networking in their offices and as communications devices between office and home, there are an estimated two to five million people who operate businesses out of their homes. The number is growing. People tired of long-distance commuting, people who realize that their dreams can become reality, people of all ages and genders are opening small businesses at home. Computer networking can greatly enhance the productivity of these businesses and become a key element in their success.

Regardless of the kind of business, personal contacts and communications remain essential. Whether you are a home decorator, financial planner, computer consultant or free-lance photographer, you have to make contact with other people for your business to thrive and prosper.

Computer technologists are already finding that bulletin boards offer a great market for their services. By posting a bulletin stating the nature of his work—accounting programs for small businesses—Mark was able to contact enough clients to ensure that his fledgling business was off to a good start.

Many other home businesses can find customers in a similar way. Advertising on local bulletin boards is free, reaches a diverse, geographically widespread and affluent group of people, and takes very little time and effort on your part. If you subscribe to a large utility, your opportunities immediately increase. Most of the utilities have no objection to your posting notices of goods and services for sale on their bulletin boards.

The Source, CompuServe and Delphi allow you to select the type of audience you wish to address. By looking at the subscriber list and selecting your most likely prospects by region, profession, hobby and other criteria, you can close in on your target and increase your odds of finding willing buyers.

Through the utilities' electronic mail services, you can contact the people you want to reach, say what you have to say and get responses quickly. Even if your prospects are not all members of the utility, you can still send your message via E-COM, MCI Mail, Mailgrams or other electronic mail services.

Special interest groups offer all kinds of possibilities for people working out of their homes. Besides contacting potential customers, you have a valuable opportunity to learn more about your business. Within each profession there are various functions and different ways of accomplishing the same goal. By talking to people who do the same sort of things that you do, you can learn what has worked for them and what has not, and how they have made their businesses more successful.

Working at home has innumerable benefits, but these do not include the chance to share your thoughts with coworkers. Most home businesses start out with one person, a good idea and a lot of hard work. Only after the business is a success do others become involved. With electronic networking, you can gain the benefit of others' ideas and experience while still in your beginning stages. By going to one of the network areas that focuses on your particular business, you can enter into conversations that will be of great value as you do your work. There is even a SIG on CompuServe dedicated to people who work at home. Accessed by "GO HOM-146," the Work-At-Home SIG concentrates on the benefits and problems that people face every day and offers those who work at home a chance to share their ideas and experiences.

Paul and Sarah Edwards of Sierra Madre, California, started the Work-At-Home SIG on CompuServe because they were interested in meeting other entrepreneurs like themselves. More than 3,500 people have joined the SIG from all over the world. The SIG provides direct communication with other people doing business out of their homes as well as many resources which would not otherwise be available to a small-business person. Listings of conferences, names and addresses of other entrepreneurs, tips on life and health insurance and other areas of special interest to people who work out of their homes are offered by the SIG.

To extend the efficiency of the network, the Edwards are forming the Association for Electronic Cottagers that will hold annual conferences and do much the same things that the SIG does except in person rather than on-line.

The utilities offer other services for people working at home. Both CompuServe and The Source offer subscribers a broad range of financial and business services. You can use one of their programs to do planning that might otherwise require a large investment in software and training. You can do your budget on-line; compute your taxes; calculate depreciation, cashflow and amortization of loans; and many other financial tasks that would otherwise require you to invest in many dollars' worth of software.

Business News

To keep you up to date on the business world in general, several utilities offer current business news. Dow Jones News Retrieval Service is strictly for the business person who wants up-to-the-minute news. CompuServe and The Source both provide access to national newspapers and news services that provide news more quickly than even your local newspaper.

Several professional organizations are also setting up their own business networks so their members can stay current on news in their special fields of interest. A writers' group in Texas is forming an alliance with a regional utility to provide free-lance writers access to information as well as to other writers, editors and people in publishing. This system allows writers to find out which magazines want free-lance material, which editors are looking for help, which publications don't pay and any other information they might want to share. It also serves as a meeting place for people who share the same professional interests. It is a boon both to writers looking for work and editors looking for workers.

Practical Connections

Whatever your profession, networking can add new dimensions to your business life. William, a farmer in Attica, Indiana, bought a personal computer to take care of his business finances. He began programming and discovered a way that his computer could help determine the temperature of the grain in his silo. As he grew more familiar with his computer, the more convinced he became that it could perform a number of functions. Remembering how, as a boy, he had heard his father and other farmers talking and was impressed with the wealth of information they had to share, he established a network of farmers who use their computers to share information. He looks forward to the day when farmers from all over the world can share information and work out their problems with people who understand their situation.

During the summer of 1983, physicians used CompuServe's MEDSIG to keep track of an important medical conference held in Europe. Those who were not able to attend the conference were given regular bulletins on-line. Those who did attend kept in touch with their offices and staffs while they were away. Future conferences will also provide networking options for doctors who are equipped to take advantage of them.

Many physicians use networks to call into databases when a puzzling or difficult case requires additional information. Because consultation with experts is not readily available to many medical practitioners, the networks are often lifesavers. A doctor can search the literature for articles dealing with a particular problem or consult on-line with other doctors to find answers.

Another imaginative use of networks in the medical field involves a small-town emergency medical service. The paramedic, often hampered by a lack of information when he arrived at the scene of a medical emergency, mounted his own TRS-100 on the dashboard of his ambulance. Using the built-in modem, he can now call up the local hospital or EMS database and get essential information about his patient. People in the community have become enthusiastic about the new system and have voluntarily sent in data about existing medical conditions, drug allergies, blood types and anything else that might be pertinent, such as directions to a hard-to-find address. As a result, the paramedic arrives at his destination ready to administer the appropriate aid.

Medical professionals are not the only ones using networks to do their jobs efficiently. A bulletin board set up by Michael Smelser focuses on law enforcement and offers the police an opportunity to tap into the network for a variety of purposes. They can exchange ideas on any aspect of law enforcement, such as reconstructing accidents and identifying suspects. The BBS is free to anyone associated with law enforcement; nonprofessionals can join for a nominal fee. As you may have guessed, Michael has publicized his service by networking. He has posted notices on national utilities to help interested people find out about his service; he makes his profit from selling hardware and software to members of his group.

CompuServe's Services For Professionals area, "GO SFP," also offers a good way to network with people in your business. Containing both bulletin board and conference options, SFP gives you a way to discuss your business with people who understand and can offer suggestions or assistance. The SFP area contains these choices.

1. AVIATION
2. COMMUNICATIONS/DATA PROCESSING
3. ENGINEERING/TECHNICAL
4. ENVIRONMENTAL
5. LEGAL
6. MEDICAL
7. JEWELERS

Sell at Home

If you have a product to sell, you may want to consider on-line sales options. Comp-U-Card International, Inc., of Stamford, Connecticut, and Viewtron, a Florida-based service of Viewdata Corporation of America, Inc., as well as Comp-U-Store, offer consumers a wide range of merchandise. Viewtron and Comp-U-Store offer shopping services for subscribers who pay a monthly fee of $30 to receive the service along with local news, weather and sports. Subscribers connect a special videotex keypad to their TV sets and a color graphics catalogue appears on the screen. They can then browse through the merchandise until what they are looking for appears on the screen. The terminal is not a personal computer; it merely allows access to the merchandise.

J. C. Penney's catalogue is on the Viewtron system along with florists, furniture dealers, booksellers and many other vendors. Terminals are available in some stores as well as to people at home. If you have a product to sell but are not interested in setting up a retail outlet, selling on-line through a shopping service may be the answer. A clothing dealer in Florida is selling clothing without opening stores or making any investment other than the fees charged by the service. Fees range from $5,000 to $50,000 per year.

Comp-U-Store is always looking for suppliers who can provide products at low prices. Because the on-line services actually hold no merchandise, they act as conduits for business and consumers to get together. Comp-U-Store will describe your product to personal-computer owners, but does not use graphics to show the products. Depending on your market and your product, one of these systems might mean the difference between a profitable and unprofitable year.

Personal Business Connections

Taking care of your personal business is also easier with electronic networks. Keeping track of investments, stocks and bonds, and making decisions about future investments is greatly simplified when you have the information available on networks. Dow Jones provides up to the minute stock prices and other information on hundreds of companies around the world. If you are thinking of investing, you can get current, reliable information on which to base your decision.

Dow Jones

Dow Jones was begun as a purely financial database, but it has evolved to offer some of the services that the information utilities provide, such as electronic mail and information exchange between users. DJNS draws information from *The Wall Street Journal* and *Barron's,* making available news in over 80 categories, information on over 6,000 companies and data on more than 50 industries. Whatever your business, one of the Dow Jones news services will have relevant information.

In addition to business news, DJNS offers the World Report from UPI. Front-page, national and foreign news stories are made available as soon as they break. Weather around the world is another service. Relatively new additions are movie reviews, sports reports and Comp-U-Store.

Of great interest to business people is Dow Jones's on-line comprehensive financial information from the New York Stock Exchange, American Stock Exchange, Midwest Stock Exchange and Pacific Stock Exchange. Stocks, money market price quotes, bonds, mutual funds and U.S. Treasury issues are included in the quotations. There is a mandatory fifteen-minute delay while trading is in progress, but unless you are on the floor of the exchange, there is no quicker way to get current prices than by calling into DJNS.

Dow Jones also enables you to track the growth of a company by checking historical quotes, using the corporate-earning estimator and accessing data filed with the Securities and Exchange Commission. The Media General DataBank offers over 60 different statistics on each of thousands of individual companies, including composite data on industry groups.

Several options are available to the experienced and beginning financier on DJNS. Many investors have found they can save money by doing their own research rather than paying a full-service brokerage house. Once they have decided on a purchase, they can arrange it through a discount brokerage firm. Whether you are managing a complex stock portfolio or making your first tentative venture into the market, the process is much easier with the services of Dow Jones at your fingertips.

NewsNet

Another service of special interest to business people is NewsNet. NewsNet offers hundreds of industry-specific newsletters on-line, minutes after the articles are written. Much of the information contained in industry newsletters can affect your business. Knowing about the information quickly can be to your benefit; finding out about it too late can cause real problems. All newsletters in NewsNet are available to subscribers to the service, whether or not they subscribe to the print versions. Additionally, all the newsletters can be searched by key words so you can find out if your business is mentioned in any related newsletters.

NewsNet offers newsletters in more than 50 industries, and the number is growing. Some of the publications include daily updates on time-sensitive matters like pricing, legislation and contracts. Unlike databases, NewsNet provides the full text of each article in the newsletters. You can read, scan, search by key word, write letters to the editors and order services or products among other options.

You pay no subscription fee when you join NewsNet, but there is a minimum usage fee of $15 per month. Connect charges at 300 baud are $24 per hour from 8 a.m. to 8 p.m., and $6 per hour from 8 p.m. to 8 a.m. and on weekends and holidays. NewsNet is accessible by Telenet, Tymnet and Uninet, whose charges are included in the NewsNet charge. Charges for reading a newsletter vary from $24 to $120 per hour, as they are set by the publisher. Subscribers to the print version of the newsletter get reduced rates for reading the publication on-line. Rates are doubled if you are receiving the service at 1200 baud. If you have a printer, however, it may actually save you money to call in at 1200 baud, print the newsletter and read it off-line. You can rent a Scanset terminal or 3M Whisper Writer from NewsNet if you do not have a communicating machine of your own but just can't wait to read their newsletters. For information call (800) 345-1301 (in Pennsylvania, (215) 527-8030).

CompuServe

CompuServe's Business and Financial Services section offers many choices that are yours for a minor investment and a few keystrokes ("GO FIN-1").

BUSINESS AND FINANCIAL SERVICES
1. NEWS/REPORTS
2. REFERENCE DATABASES
3. COMMUNICATIONS
4. BROKERAGE SERVICES
5. BANKING SERVICES
6. DISCUSSION FORUM
7. TRAVEL SERVICES
8. PERSONAL FINANCE

News is also available in the CNS section on items ranging from cattle or metal-futures prices to the weather in Asia, in case you want to travel there to sell your cattle and metals.

Besides the abundance of data available to the electronic networker, there is the opportunity of talking directly and inexpensively with people with whom you do business. Even with connect charges, $6 per hour is much cheaper than a phone call, and you can record the conversation. During regular working hours an electronic conference with people in many different places is a bargain. Travel time and expense need no longer stand in the way. By using any of the conference options provided by the utilities, you can hold your meeting regardless of the locations of participants.

Looking for a Job?

But what if you're looking for work? No problem. Electronic networking will come to your aid. The Source has a career network, accessed by the key word "EMPLOY," that is designed specifically for those who are looking for new jobs. Job categories listed in the network range from Accounting to Utilities and include such diverse fields as Education, Construction, the Arts and Industry. There is also a place to leave your resume so that when a prospective employer comes on-line it will be right there for him or her to consider.

Getting a job through a network is not uncommon. Sometimes the employer posts a bulletin:

"Jones and Loki are seeking a part-time art director for our advertising department. We need someone who has experience with print and television media and is willing to work flexible hours. If you are interested, leave electronic mail for 7777,777 (Charlene Loki)."

Other times, the prospective employee leaves a message:

"Do you need a graphic designer? I have 12 years' experience with a small advertising agency, designing ads, logos, publications and letterheads. I'm interested in working part-time while I work on my novel. Contact me at 4444,444 (Jack Loofa)."

Other networks offer opportunities for those looking for employees and those looking for employment to meet and discuss things to their mutual advantage.

Besides specifically job-oriented networks, general networks also provide good career opportunities. People often find jobs by talking with friends and acquaintances in the course of their daily lives. The same is true when people communicate regularly through electronic networks. Several free-lance writers have established contact with editors and publishers through conversations in literary special interest groups. Other people have become friends through the CB Simulator and learned of job opportunities they would never otherwise have known about. Just as job opportunities crop up in daily conversation, they crop up in electronic conversation. The major difference is that the field of possibilities is a lot wider.

11

Who Won the World Series in 1948?

Databases

Do you need to know an obscure fact? Is your teenager struggling with a report on Polish agriculture? Does your college professor expect you to know everything about Planck's work in physics? Do you need background on an investment? Are you involved in professional research? If there's anything you need to know, you can find the answer from one of the hundreds of online databases available to the electronic networker.

One of the important aspects of education is learning how to find the information you need. No one is expected to know everything. The key is being able to find out what you want to know in the shortest time.

A database is a storage tank for facts. Hundreds of thousands, often millions of pieces of data are stored in the tank, and the tank has the ability to pick out precisely the pieces you need and present them to you. Try to imagine a huge tank full of fish, all swimming around in the water. Each of the fish has a word or words written on its back. You, being a particular sort of fish fancier, want only the fish that say "crimson" and "cyclamen." You bend over the tank, shout your two words, and as if by magic all the crimson and cyclamen fish come up to see you.

That's how a database works. You can't actually see all the pieces of data floating around, and you can't just shout to make them rise to the surface, but it's almost that simple.

Databases can contain any kind of data. They can be catalogues of newspaper articles, lists of books in print, medical reference texts, sports records, or weather forecasts. They can be encyclopedias, stock market transactions, or names and addresses of famous people. What distinguishes databases from other kinds of computer data is that the data can be sorted and selected in a variety of ways. For example, suppose you have a database with this record in it:

LAST NAME—PURVIS
FIRST NAME—GWENDOLYN
MIDDLE NAME—EMERITUS
PROFESSION—PEANUT BUTTER TASTER
HOBBY1—MOUNTAIN CLIMBING
HOBBY2—FLOWER PRESSING
HOBBY3—ADVANCED CALCULUS
CITY—OMAHA
STATE—NEBRASKA
COMPUTER—IBM JR.
AUTOMOBILE—PACKARD
MARITALSTATUS—BIGAMIST

If you dip into the database that contains this entry, you can find Gwendolyn any number of ways. You can ask for everyone who lives in Omaha and find her. You can ask for everyone who enjoys mountain climbing and find her. You can even ask for everyone whose middle name is Emeritus and find her. You don't have to know that she is there to begin with; you just have to know the sort of person you are looking for. If you are interested in finding all the people who are bigamist Packard drivers, the database will provide you dear Gwendolyn's data.

Your field can be as broad or as narrow as you wish. By selecting several things to define your search, you will end up with more specific data. Obviously, if you ask for everyone in Nebraska you will end up with a longer list than if you ask for every peanut butter taster in Omaha.

There are on-line databases that provide data for almost every need. Whether you just want a fact for your own information or are involved in a serious research project, databases can provide the data you need. If you have ever done any sort of research in a library, you know how time-consuming the process can be. First you have to go through the listings—whether they are card catalogues, microfiche records or periodical guides. Once you have found where to look, you have hours ahead of digging through books, magazines, encyclopedias, and articles. The process can seem—and be—interminable. The greatest benefit of on-line databases is that they can save you great amounts of time. In addition, you can be pretty sure that your research has been thorough.

Databases on National Utilities

How serious you want to get in your research will determine which databases you will want to use. For general purposes, you can usually find what you need on CompuServe, The Source or Delphi. Each of those utilities has on-line newspapers and stock reports to keep you up-to-date and to provide current data on a wide range of topics.

CompuServe has a Reference Library section which can help on many subjects.

REFERENCE LIBRARY

1. ACADEMIC AMER. ENCYCLOPEDIA
2. INFORMATION ON DEMAND
3. U.S. GOVERNMENT PUBLICATIONS
4. BIBLIOGRAPHIC SERVICES

5. FAMILY	6. FASHION
7. GARDENING	8. GOLF
9. DEVELOPMENT	10. SCIENCE
11. SATIRE	12. SEXUALITY

13. WINE
14. THE NEW TECH TIMES

The Source also offers News & Reference Resources as well as Business and Financial Markets:

NEWS & REFERENCE RESOURCES (1)

1. NEWS & SPORTS (UPI)
2. TRAVEL & DINING
3. GOVERNMENT & POLITICS
4. CONSUMER INFORMATION
5. BYLINES NEWS FEATURES

BUSINESS/FINANCIAL MARKETS (2)

1. FINANCIAL MARKETS
2. ANALYSIS & COMPUTATION
3. NEWS & COMMENTARY
4. PERSONAL FINANCE
5. RESEARCH & REFERENCE

The three general interest utilities also have on-line encyclopedias for reference. Delphi includes The Kussmaul Encyclopedia, plus The Research Library, a collection of 200 databases with comprehensive information on just about everything, and The Dialcom Library, which focuses on technical services. A special feature of Delphi is the Dear Oracle section. By asking the Oracle a question, you can get quick answers from other members about a subject that interests you. Probably someone there actually knows who won the World Series in 1948!

DIALOG

Delphi also serves as a gateway to the DIALOG databases. DIALOG, a subsidiary of Lockheed Missile and Space Co., offers over 150 individual databases ranging from ABI/INFORM, business-related articles published since 1971, to ZOOLOGICAL RECORD, data from 6,000 journals published worldwide about our furry, feathery and scaly friends. In the middle are databases dealing with education for your exceptional child, foundation grants, abstracts from the *Congressional Record* and world textiles. DIALOG is the largest database system in the U.S.

DIALOG is an "encyclopedic database," which means that it contains sub-databases on a wide range of topics. Just as a printed encyclopedia includes information of all types, so does an encyclopedic database. It is made up of many single-subject databases, each of which is called up separately. All encyclopedic databases have a "search" language that you must use to tell the computer what you want. The languages range in simplicity from fairly simple to pretty hard, but once you learn the language you can use it on any database in the system. Any use of an encyclopedic database should first be preceded by a bit of time spent learning the language and figuring out a plan of action.

Because these databases are so comprehensive and powerful, they are not cheap to use. You can subscribe directly or use your Delphi subscription to enter DIALOG. In either case, there is an additional charge for time spent in a database. The charges range from $25 to $300 per hour, depending on which database you are using. Remember, however, that you are charged only for the time you use; if you plan your visit well, you can accomplish a great deal in 15 minutes.

To get information from most databases, you type in key words. If you are a doctor, for example, and call up DIALOG's Medline database for information about the effects of rubella on unborn infants, you can type in the words "RUBELLA AND EMBRYOS" and the database will give you a list of articles. Each article you get will contain data on both rubella and embryos; you won't get general articles about rubella with no reference to embryos. You can narrow your field further by specifying rubella, embryos, and vaccine, or widen it to include children and infants, depending on your needs.

Databases generally do not contain the complete text of all articles. What they do give you is a bibliography of books and articles, including a brief abstract of each article. If you are using a database that includes newspapers, you are more likely to find whole stories, or at least a summary of each article mentioned. Reference texts, like the encyclopedias that the utilities provide, do have complete articles for you to read and gather information from without having to make a trip to the library.

If you locate an article that you would like to read but only a summary is on the database, most systems allow you to request a photocopy of the complete article. You can complete the transaction on-line. Of course, you have to pay extra for the service. You can also print the results of your search on- or off-line. If you print it on-line, it is in your hands immediately. Having it printed and sent to you takes longer but minimizes connect time.

Knowledge Index

Another DIALOG option is the Knowledge Index. Probably of more interest to the general user, the Knowledge Index is a selection of DIALOG's consumer-oriented databases, accessible in the evenings and on weekends. Usage fee is a flat rate of $24 per hour, plus the $35 subscription fee. There is no minimum charge for monthly service; you pay only for the time you use. Unless you are doing in-depth research in a specialized area, this service can meet most of your needs. Subject areas include business, books, psychology, magazines, computer information and engineering. Knowledge Index is accessible Monday through Thursday, 6 p.m. to 5 a.m. (your time); Friday, 6 p.m. to midnight; Saturday 8 a.m. to midnight; and Sunday 3 p.m. to 5 a.m. The start-up fee includes a self-instructional manual that provides all the information you need to begin using the system. Two free hours of usage are also included in the start-up. Telecommunications charges are included in the hourly connect fee. Knowledge Index also provides customer assistance from 7 p.m. to 11 p.m. (EST) weeknights at (800) 227-5510, or (415) 858-3796 in California.

Searching in the Knowledge Index is done by key words. A typical search looks like this:

    ? BEGIN COMPUTERS AND ELECTRONICS (You select the database you want to use. In this case it is called Computers and Electronics.)

    ? FIND PERSONAL COMPUTER AND ENERGY CONSERVATION (You are interested in articles which mention both computers and energy conservation.)

    440 PERSONAL COMPUTER

    699 ENERGY CONSERVATION

    S1 2 PERSONAL COMPUTER AND ENERGY CONSERVATION (The system is telling you that there are 440 articles about personal computers, 699 articles about energy conservation and 2 articles about both. S1 means that this is your first search of the session.)

    ? DISPLAY S1 (This tells the computer to show you the first item it found on your search.)

    ENERGY CONSERVATION WITH A MICROCOMPUTER

JACKSON,D.R.; CALAHAN, J.M.
UNIV. OF CONNECTICUT ENERGY
CENTER,STORRS,CT,USA
BYTE (USA) VOL.6 NO.7 178-208 JULY 1981
DOCUMENT TYPE: JOURNAL PAPER
(4 REFS)
PRESENTS SEVERAL TOOLS THAT CAN BE USED
IN CONJUNCTION....

The computer has told you everything you need to know about this article: title, author, name of periodical, date, and finally a summary of the article. You can then order a complete text of the article to be mailed to you, go to the library and find the magazine referenced, or decide you weren't really interested in the subject after all. This search, which covered over half a million citations drawn from 2,300 journals and magazines, took less than two minutes and cost a grand total of 74 cents.

DIALOG is headquartered in Palo Alto, California, and may be contacted at (800) 227-1927 or (800) 982-5838. Information on Knowledge Index is available by calling (800) 227-5510, or (415) 858-3796 in California.

BRS

Another large encyclopedic database is BRS. Located in Latham, New York, BRS is a major on-line search service that can be used in a variety of ways. If you are a professional researcher or work for a company that could use the services of BRS, there are special rates for users who call into the service frequently. Subscription plans are available to fit your budget and amount of usage, and there is an open access plan that allows you to pay as you use the system.

BRS offers eighty databases, including science, technology, medicine and many other areas of interest. To use BRS, you need to learn the search command language; BRS recommends that you take their one-day training class to become proficient in the language. The class is offered in several locations around the country. They also recommend that you use the system fairly often to maintain proficiency.

BRS/After Dark

The option that most personal computer users will select, however, is called BRS/After Dark. While BRS offers extensive data for research professionals, BRS/After Dark offers a number of options at reduced prices for those who use databases less frequently and are willing to use the system after normal business hours. Accessible from six in the evening on weekdays and around the clock on weekends and holidays, BRS/After Dark charges a one-time subscription fee of $50, plus hourly rates ranging from $6 to $20. The service can be billed to MasterCard or Visa accounts, and there is a monthly minimum charge of $12. Databases on the BRS system include business, math, science, health, psychology and family planning. The full text of the Academic American Encyclopedia and the Harvard Business Review are also on-line.

BRS/After Dark contains 30 of the most commonly used databases of general interest and is much easier to use than BRS. No training is necessary to search these databases. A software interface has been developed that prompts the user and helps the search go quickly and easily. For information about both BRS and BRS/After Dark, call Customer Service at (800) 833-4707 or (518) 783-1161.

Orbit

Another widely used encyclopedic database is Orbit, a division of SDC Information Services in Santa Monica, California. Orbit offers data in the fields of science, engineering, business, electronics and many others. It is available 22 hours a day, Monday through Friday. The subscription fee varies from $125 to $400, depending on how much training you need to learn the system. This system requires some training to become proficient in its use, but the cost will be recovered in savings of on-line charges. Rates range from $40 to $125 per hour depending on the database you are using. For information about Orbit, call (800) 421-7229 or (800) 352-6689.

Other Database Options

One valuable source of data that has not yet been widely used, but which is both inexpensive and comprehensive, is operated by the U.S. government. Because all the work was done at your expense as a taxpayer, the charge for accessing government databases is minimal. There are approximately 10,000 government databases, many available to the public. The main problem with this source is the difficulty of finding out what is there and how to get at it. Directories of on-line services, such as *Datapro, Information Sources*, and others, may be able to help you find what you need.

If the data you need are likely to be found in newspapers rather than magazines, journals or books, you'll want to look into The New York Times Information Bank. The Information Bank was started in 1969 by The New York Times company and contains the full text of *The Times*, as well as abstracts from many other publications. Special index words are added to each article to make the database easily searchable. Abstracts of articles from every issue of *The Times* from 1974 forward are on-line. In addition, The Information Bank offers abstracts from the following publications:

Newspapers:

Atlanta Constitution	*Chicago Tribune*
Christian Science Monitor	*Houston Chronicle*
Los Angeles Times	*Miami Herald*
San Francisco Chronicle	*Seattle Times*
Washington Post	

Business news:

Advertising Age	*Automotive News*
Barron's	*Business Week*
Dun's Business Month	*Editor and Publisher*
Financial Times of Canada	*Financial Times of London*
Forbes	*Fortune*
Harvard Business Review	*Japan Economic Journal*
Journal of Commerce	*Wall Street Journal*
Women's Wear Daily	

International news:

Economist (London)	*Far Eastern Economic Review*
Foreign Affairs	*Foreign Policy*
Latin American Weekly	*Manchester Guardian*
Middle East Times (London)	*World Press Review (Atlas)*

Science news:

Astronautics	*Aviation Week and Space*
Bulletin of Atomic Scientists	*Technology*
Science	*Industrial Research*
Scientific American	

Miscellaneous:

Atlantic	*California Journal*
Consumer Reports	*Current Biography*
National Journal	*National Review*
New York	*New Yorker*
Newsweek	*Sports Illustrated*
Time	*U.S. News and World Report*
Variety	*Washington Monthly*

In addition to The Information Bank, the New York Times Information Service (NYTIS) offers six other databases. New York Times Online offers the complete text of *The Times* from 1980 to the present except for ads, stock quotes and announcements.

Advertising/Marketing Intelligence, AMI, is a joint effort of NYTIS and the J. Walter Thompson advertising agency. Included in this database are advertising and marketing journals and journals dealing with public relations, broadcasting, communications, food, pharmaceuticals, retailing, product development and other topics.

SUMM is a service that provides you a summary of the day's news before it has even gotten into print. Drawn primarily from *The New York Times*, these summaries are put on-line three times daily. Their major emphasis is business news.

Deadline Data on World Affairs is a database produced by DMS, a consulting and research firm in Connecticut. This service offers full text retrieval on a huge amount of data. World population statistics, cultural information, political leaders and their positions, military data, and international organizations are among the data on-line.

Disclosure II contains weekly updates of financial statements for more than 8,000 publicly held companies. Also available on Dow Jones News Retrieval Service and DIALOG, this database provides a great deal of information for those interested in investing in or tracking the progress of a particular corporation.

Globe Data, the other database offered by NYTIS, is an index to the *Boston Globe* newspaper.

The simplest way to use NYTIS databases is by a "controlled-vocabulary" search. When you subscribe to the service, you receive a "Thesaurus," a list of key words the system uses to find articles relating to your field of interest.

Each database is priced differently; rates range from $75 to $165 an hour. In addition, you pay between $7 and $10 telecommunications charge. If you plan to use the service extensively, there are discount rates. (See Chapter 15 for phone numbers.)

There are many different databases available to the home user. Each one can offer invaluable aid if you are searching for information. The perfect one for you, however, depends on your needs and your goals. Dow Jones, Citishare Corporation, and Chase Econometrics all offer a wealth of financial and economic data and statistics. Dow Jones and Nite-Line offer financial and business data. NewsNet contains the full text of over 100 newsletters plus the options of contacting the publishers of the newsletters and sending electronic mail. ITT Dialcom contains a variety of databases, including business, government, energy and travel.

Single Subject Databases

There are also thousands of single-subject databases. If all you really want to know about is horses, you can call up a database in Lexington, Kentucky called "HORSE" and find out everything you ever wanted to know about pedigreed race horses in North America. Many of these single-subject databases are specific to a particular science, occupation or hobby. The *Directory of Online Databases,* published by Cuadra Associates of Santa Monica, California, keeps a current list of all single-subject and encyclopedic databases in the country. The *Omni Online Database Directory* also lists on-line services by subject matter and includes a description of contents, a comment from users, and names and addresses of all databases included. Other published listings will become available as enthusiasm grows for on-line research. Be sure, however, that the listing you use is current because the field is changing quickly with new databases being added regularly. Without a current list, you may miss just the database you need.

Almost anything you need to know, at whatever level of detail, is available on some database. The choice may not be easy, but it is nice to know that the choice is there. On-line databases have probably been around longer than any other service home networkers use. Holding large amounts of data and allowing it to be extracted was one of the first uses of computers. The systems are now open to people working out of their homes or offices with a small computer and modem.

Database Help

If you don't want to learn search languages or spend time doing your own research, people out there will be glad to do it for you— for a fee. By networking, you can meet the people who operate on-line search services. One such service is Computer Assisted Research On Line (C.A.R.O.L.). Located in Florida, this group will do your research on-line and get you the results quickly. One of the beautiful features of networking is that you can find all sorts of people who can help you. Bob Sherman can be called at (305) 944-2111 for further information about C.A.R.O.L.

CompuServe also has database research clinics that can help you get acquainted with this kind of research and make the process go more smoothly. If you cannot call in and attend, the clinics are kept on file for you to read at your convenience.

New hardware and software are also being developed to help you take advantage of available data. Texas Instruments, Inc. offers a software package to allow access to the Dow Jones News/Retrieval service. NaturalLink offers features that take care of dialing, signing on to the system and planning your visit and does not require that you learn DJNS's search language. You can type in all your questions before dialing into the system, and NaturalLink will automatically ask them for you once you are connected.

More of these simplifying software packages will be coming along as people use databases with greater frequency. Given the choice of calling in and getting answers in minutes or slogging through stacks of books, magazines and directories, who can doubt that the future of research is on-line?

Oh, by the way, The Cleveland Indians won the World Series in 1948, beating the Braves of Boston before they moved on to Milwaukee and then Atlanta. You could have found that out for yourself if you were already enjoying the fun of electronic networking.

12

What Else Can I Do?

A Potpourri of Electronic Services

Now that you have made friends all over the country, found a way to finish your degree in your spare time, organized your upcoming city elections and taken a lover, you're probably sitting around wondering "What else can I do?"

Never fear. The list of things you can do with your newfound networking abilities is limited only by your imagination If you are willing to take the time and trouble to set up networks, you can do practically anything. If, on the other hand, you just want to take advantage of someone else's work and use what's already out there, you still have a lot of choices.

Suppose, for example, that you've been trying to think up a novel idea for your best friend's birthday. You've already sent balloons, had dancing girls perform at his office and built a cake that looks like the Golden Gate Bridge. What's left for the innovative birthday-giver? An electronic birthday card, of course. The Friendly Bytes Company will be pleased to sell you a greeting card that will appear on your friend's computer screen complete with music and twinkling candles on the cake.

But perhaps this is a really good friend—a friend that no birthday card, no matter how flashy or musical, can truly honor; the kind of friend who deserves a tour of the Louvre—conducted by you, of course. You need to decide whether Paris is really the place you want to go, see what the airline schedule looks like and make reservations. Does this mean you have to go to a travel agent, carry away and pore through dozens of brochures, try to figure out an agreeable schedule and finally make your plans? Of course not. You are an electronic networker.

Travel Services

First of all, you need to decide on a destination and times that will be convenient for both you and your friend. You can dial up The Electronic Edition of the Official Airline Guides and get complete, up-to-the-minute information on over 700,000 scheduled flights for more than 600 airlines serving approximately 105,000 cities. The Electronic Edition is updated as soon as an airline makes any change in its schedule or rates.

Published by Official Airline Guides Inc., a Dun & Bradstreet company, The Electronic Edition is accessible through Tymnet or Telenet. You can use the service free for thirty days and then decide whether to subscribe. If you do, the cost is an initial $50 plus $6 per hour connect time, day or night. In addition, you pay thirty cents for each flight schedule and twenty cents for each fare requested. The Official Airline Guides' literature says that the "typical round-trip planning session is estimated to take seven minutes and cost $2.25."

If you are already a member of CompuServe, you can use The Electronic Edition without subscribing. There is an additional charge from CompuServe for the service, so it may be less expensive to join The Electronic Edition if you plan to use it often.

After you've decided where you want to go, or if you were sure about the Louvre in the first place, you need a way to make quick, easy, guaranteed reservations. You need a travel agent, but not just any travel agent. You need an electronic travel agent. If you subscribe to CompuServe or The Source, you already have one. First Travel of Coronado, California is the electronic travel agent for both services. All you have to do is call up your network, select the travel option and tell them where you want to go, when you want to go, where you want to stay, whether you need a car, and any other little details you want taken care of. You will get an immediate reply, either by voice phone or on your computer, whichever you choose. Your reservations will be made and charged to your credit card without your ever having to leave your terminal. If you make your reservations early enough, your tickets will be mailed to you. If not, you can pick them up at the ticket counter when you check your baggage.

Now that's a really simple, time-saving way to plan a birthday party. All you have to do is get to the airport, brush up your French (probably through some electronic teaching aid) and remember which is Monet and which is Manet.

Electronic Publishing

Once you have taken off on your trip, you'll probably want to keep a record of your adventures and make the thrilling story available to your public. On-line publishing is your best bet for getting your words read. Whether you choose to write sonnets about your travels or a full-scale travelogue, you can put your work on-line for hundreds of people to read. Most national utilities have places for publishing, as do many regional and local bulletin boards. All you need to do is determine your target audience and hook up your modem. You can even send it day by day as you travel around so everyone can keep up with what is going on.

Shopping Services

Let's suppose, however, that this friend is a good friend, but not that good. You like him well enough to spend some money on a nice gift, but not enough to take him to Paris. Your handy network is there to help. You can go shopping electronically with the ease of pushing a few buttons. No crowds, no grouchy clerks, no traffic jams or rock music in the malls. In the privacy of your own terminal you can buy Godiva chocolates, crystal aperitif glasses, a printer for his new computer, or a dozen long-stemmed red roses.

If you are looking for a really elegant gift—say an island in the Caribbean or an antique Persian rug or a nifty little personalized jet—you'll want to sign on with the Collector's Data Service. Located in Seattle, Washington, this service caters to the collector of fine art, antiques and exotic and expensive items. Included in their listing are aircraft, antiques, coins, exotic real estate, gems, horses, purebred pets and rare books and stamps. Collector's Data Service has no membership fees, minimums or monthly charges. It is accessible by a local Tymnet number and the only charges are for connect time. The charges are $16.80 per hour from 7 a.m. to 6 p.m., and $8.40 per hour other times.

You can also use Collector's Data Service to list your old Renoir's or that yacht you've grown tired of. In addition to listings, the service offers category newsletters, auction schedules and prices, glossaries of key terms, events calendars, stolen property lists and show dates. For information, call (800) 435-0100 (in Seattle, Washington, (206) 281-7273).

Dow Jones, CompuServe and The Source offer at-home shopping to subscribers. Comp-U-Store, the largest on-line shopping service in the country, can be accessed through the major utilities. It offers over 60,000 items and more than 200 major brands—appliances, cameras, flatware, luggage, sporting goods, stereo equipment, TVs, video and electronic equipment, watches, computer products and a lot more. You can choose to get information on all the listings of your product or just one brand. If you are shopping for a camera, for instance, you can look at all the cameras offered, or just Canons.

Membership fees to Comp-U-Store are $25 for one year or $40 for two years and include a user number, manual and VISA application. In Comp-U-Store, you can either use your credit card or pay in advance by check or money order. (These charges are in addition to connect time charged by the utility.)

Comp-U-Store offers all its items at a discount, so the amount you spend on-line can be made up in reduced prices. Discounts range from ten to forty percent off the manufacturer's suggested retail price; prices include shipping. Each product carries the same warranty you would expect if you bought the item in a store. When you enter Comp-U-Store, you will see this menu:

    (1) HELP & INFORMATION
    (2) SHOPPING & ORDERING
    (3) TO PROCESS A STORED ORDER
    (4) DATABASEMENT (BARGAINS)
    (5) COMP-U-STAKES (AUCTION)

The manual you receive will help you with commands and procedures for ordering and shopping. As with most on-line services, it is advisable to plan your shopping spree before you call. You can save time and money by familiarizing yourself with the system and the commands off-line.

In addition to Comp-U-Store, most utilities offer their own shopping services. When you buy an item from one of these, it is charged to your credit card along with your connect charges. CompuServe offers ten separate shopping services. Typing "GO HOM-40" will let you see a listing.

There are several places to shop in CompuServe. Howard Sams deals in books, with an emphasis on technical and computer books. The Athlete's Outfitter, as you might guess, sells sporting goods and clothing for your athletic outings. The Music Information Service specializes in printed music, musical instruments and accessories, records and tapes. If you are an old-radio-show buff, you can choose from over 1,000 cassette recordings of radio classics of the 30s, 40s and 50s. AutoNet does not actually sell you anything, but it does make shopping for an automobile a lot more organized and efficient. The system is set up to let you compare features of over 350 current car models, so that when you are ready to purchase you'll know exactly what you're buying.

Finally, there is Fifth Avenue Shopper. This is a good place to look for that gift for your friend. Elegance and class are the keynotes here. Godiva chocolates, books, perfumes and crystal are among the items you can choose. You can even have them ship fresh flowers almost anywhere in the world.

If you use The Source, you can shop in the Catalog Shopping area.

CATALOG SHOPPING
1. DATA BUCKS
2. BARTER
3. BOOKS
4. RECORDS, TAPES, VIDEOTAPES
5. RADIO RECORDINGS
6. CLASSIFIED ADS
7. COMP-U-STORE

The second option, BARTER, may be of interest if you have something you'd like to trade for something else. A service of Barter Worldwide, Inc., *Tradenet* offers a way for people to exchange items to their mutual benefit. If you want to acquire a certain item or have something you'd like to trade, you can list it in this section. Once you are listed, you are given a client number and your information is included in the database. People who enter the Barter section can search the listings by key words to find items of interest.

Services as well as goods can be exchanged on the barter system. Among the items included are accounting services, computer terminals, dentistry, films, investigation, mobile telephones, picture frames, resort accomodations, and warehousing. Once an exchange is arranged, Barter Worldwide charges a commission of ten percent of the cash value. Each item listed must retail for at least $500.

CompuServe's Electronic Mall debuted in the spring of 1984 and offers shoppers items from eighty retailers and manufacturers. A joint effort of CompuServe and L.M. Berry & Company, The Mall contains eleven shopping areas, each one representing a particular type of product and group of merchants:

Book Bazaar—books are offered for sale from a variety of publishers, with special emphasis on computer books. Catalogues including *dilithium Press, McGraw-Hill Books, Small Computer Book Club,* and *Waldenbooks* provide a wide range of choices. All books are offered at discount prices.

Photo Booth—*47th Street Photo,* offers discount photographic and electronics supplies. Cameras, lenses, lighting and darkroom supplies are among the items available

Micro Mart—offers a wide choice of microcomputers and computer products from catalogues of hardware and software dealers and manufacturers across the country, including Commodore, Sears, Digital Equipment and Inmac.

Gardening Shed—Stark Bros. catalogue offers plants, trees, and gardening supplies for green thumb enthusiasts.

Record Emporium—a catalogue from Record World will let you choose from over 5,000 record titles, or you can join any of several record clubs in this section.

Newsstand—subscribe to the *Asian Wall Street Journal, Christian Science Monitor, National Business Employment Weekly,* or any of several publications to keep abreast of the news.

Software Shop—major software distributors and publishers offer their wares in catalogues that are searchable in a variety of ways.

A special feature, "Ask Mr. Software," lets you access an on-line hotline to give expert advice and answer questions.

Financial Market—insurance and financial companies in this market can help you evaluate your decisions before you make them. E.F. Hutton's on-line brokerage service and banking services are also included.

Magazine Kiosk—browse through magazines or subscribe to your favorites in numerous subject areas.

Travel Agency—Hertz, American Airlines, and American Express have all set up shop here to make planning your travels simple and speedy. Other features make the experience stress-free.

The General Store—everything else you can think of is here. Sears, American Express and Bloomingdale's all have catalogues that you can peruse at the touch of a button. You can even order printed catalogues if you want to do your shopping that way.

Having been on your shopping spree (unless you decided to trade your ski outfit for a week at a seaside resort), you'll probably need to check your bank account and see whether you need to apply for that evening job or not. You don't have to leave the comfort of CompuServe to do that.

Banking Services

CompuServe and other utilities offer on-line banking. CompuServe has four banks on-line: First Tennessee Bank in Knoxville, Tennessee; the Huntington National Bank in Columbus, Ohio; Shawmut Bank of Boston, Massachusetts; and the Central Trade Bank in Memphis, Tennessee. Since you will be conducting all your business electronically, it is not even necessary that your bank be near your home.

The banks all provide bill-paying, checking and savings accounts, complete with statements, and some other services. If you have your paycheck automatically deposited, you will have quick access to your money. The banks can also be instructed to send you a specified amount for cash or transfer funds to a local bank for your cash needs.

A few banks have set up their own networks for customers to tap into from their homes. Pronto, Chemical Bank's home banking system, charges customers $12 per month to use the electronic banking option. The bank keeps track of all checks paid, notes when they cleared the account, and maintains a running balance. For those of us whose check register always looks like Egyptian hieroglyphics, this feature alone may be worth the $12 service charge.

Bank of America, Citibank, Chase Manhattan and Manufacturers Hanover Trust Company also offer home banking systems for their customers. Some of the banking systems allow communication between customer and bank and with fellow customers through a sort of bulletin board option. There is also talk of broadening the banking services by adding entertainment, shopping and reservation services. So far, however, most of the private bank systems are still in the development and testing stages to determine what their customers want and how they want to use the system.

Electronic Flea Markets

But suppose you check your bank account and discover that, sad but true, the cupboard is bare. Then you can have an electronic garage sale. You can do this on almost any system you want. Local bulletin boards are good places to sell unwanted items. Everything from water beds to modems is for sale on BBSs, and people who post these listings are generally pleased with the results. Computer-related items do especially well, but people have also sold cars, cameras, and many other things.

If you really want to increase your marketplace, post your "for sale" sign on a national utility. These boards are read by thousands of people, one of whom is bound to need what you have. Of course if you are selling your old sofa bed and someone two thousand miles away wants to buy it, delivery may eat into your profits dramatically. However, if you are selling small items that are easily sent by mail— perhaps Aunt Zena's favorite gingerbread recipe—the bigger your market, the bigger your profit. The posting costs you almost nothing and the responses you get may surprise you.

Software Shopping

With all the money you make from your sale, you might even have a little left over for a present for yourself. If you are in the market for software, you will want to check into Searchmart Corporation's free-access software library. There are several databases that include software in their offerings, but none can match the price of Searchmart. Free to users, Searchmart's on-line system lists, describes and demonstrates thousands of individual applications and systems software packages. You can select the programs that do what you want done and that are compatible with your own system.

Searchmart is not a buying service, but a shopping service. With the many new programs that are being developed daily, it's difficult to keep up with what's what. This service can save a great deal of shopping and confusion by letting you know immediately what is available. For more information, call Searchmart at (305) 845-2996.

If you are looking for software and have a CP/M-based machine, you may want to check into *DataCast* magazine. An article by Tony Bove and Kelly Smith shows how to access and download more than 2,400 free CP/M programs. Remote CP/M systems (RCPM) are set up to help you accomplish this goal, and the article gives you complete and clear instructions. It also includes a directory of RCPM systems throughout the U.S. and Canada. The magazine is published bimonthly, and the issue to order containing Bove and Smith's article is number 004.

Teleconferencing

Teleconferencing sounds like something only heads of state or giant corporations would do with any regularity. However, it is neither difficult nor inaccessible to the home computer networker. Teleconferencing is another word for people using a network to talk about a specific subject. There are many conferences in progress on-line at all times. All you have to do to become a participant is to join in.

PARTI, short for "Participate," is a feature of The Source, and one of the oldest and most active conferencing methods around. However, the Electronic Information Exchange System, is the original conferencing system. Developed in 1975 by Murray Turrof with a grant from the National Science Foundation, EIES (pronounced "eyes") is a software system that allows conferencing to go on for years without any of the comments being lost. Conferences can be either open to all subscribers or private.

Anyone on the system can initiate a computer conference. If you have a topic that interests you and on which you'd like others to add their thoughts or expertise, you can begin a conference. All you have to do is tell the system that you want to start a conference, give it a title, and write a short description of the conference for others to read and decide whether they'd like to join.

Say, for example, that you'd like to start a conference on the use of herbs. You tell the computer that you want to start a new conference called HERBLORE. Then you enter your introduction:

"I have been studying herbs for several years and am fascinated with the many uses they have—ranging from medicinal to aphrodisiacal. This conference will center on uses people have found for herbs, the best places to find fresh herbs, and ways of producing, storing, and preparing herbs."

At this point you can either enter the first message in the conference or wait for someone else to join. Perhaps Martha will come along and say, "I've been using comfrey ointment, which I buy, for several years for skin abrasions and other minor irritations. Does anyone know how to make the ointment using fresh comfrey?"

Jack, who calls in a couple of hours later, knows just what to do, leaves Martha the ointment recipe, and adds a bit more information to the list. The benefit of this system is that it helps you zero in on topics of real interest to you. Each entry is kept on file for new users to read, and many people can benefit from one person's knowledge. Martha gets her recipe, and anyone else may use it as well.

Usually, when you first enter a conference you will want to read the comments that have gone before. Once you are up to date with these notices, the computer will keep track of your visits and tell you what has been added since your last visit. That saves your having to keep a diary of notices you've read.

Other options are available to computer conferencers. PARTI and EIES allow you to search for conferences by keywords contained in their subject lines. Electronic mail, voting, word-processing capability, and a list of those on-line at the same time as you are among the options offered. If you find someone who is on-line while you are, you can make direct contact with them and carry on a real time miniconference.

EIES limits its membership and therefore is less widely used than PARTI on The Source. PARTI is designed to be simple to use, but, as with most systems, you will have to get used to the commands. The Source provides an opportunity to do this by allowing first-time users to enter a practice conference. This exercise will guide you through the conference mode, and, by the time you are finished, you will be ready to join one of the ongoing conferences.

The subject matter of conferences is unlimited. Anything that interests anyone is a likely topic for a conference. EIES contains conferences on poetry, French, graffiti, privacy, religion, politics and many other subjects. PARTI offers an even larger number of ongoing conferences, most of which are open to any interested subscriber. The Participate system required over ten years to develop, and attention has been paid to convenience and user friendliness. Developed by Chandler Harrison Stevens, Participate is available only on The Source, and there is no extra charge for its use.

Conferences are also available to CompuServe and Delphi subscribers. Although most conferences are open to the public, you can hold a private meeting on-line. Perhaps you'd like to have a meeting of the planning group for your 25th high school reunion. Obviously this is private, top-secret stuff. You don't want just anyone barging in and suggesting you make a giant number 25 with chicken wire and Kleenex. What you need is a private conference. Each of the committee members can call in at a prearranged time, the conversation can be scrambled so that no one else can hear the plans, or the conference can be closed except to those who know the password. Your plans can be made, assignments handed out and the party well on its way to success, probably for less than $10. It doesn't even matter that the members of the committee have moved to half a dozen different points on the globe.

The ability to confer over great distances with people you may not even know yet is a recurring wonder of electronic networks. What you can do with this ability is limited only by your imagination. You can set up an exercise class with your three best friends in Miami, Los Angeles and Fairbanks. You can send your manuscript to your publisher while he is attending a sales conference in the

Bahamas. You can write home to Mother while you are doing The Grand Tour. What else can you do? Just about anything you want to do! As long as you have a phone line and a communicating machine, the sky's the limit.

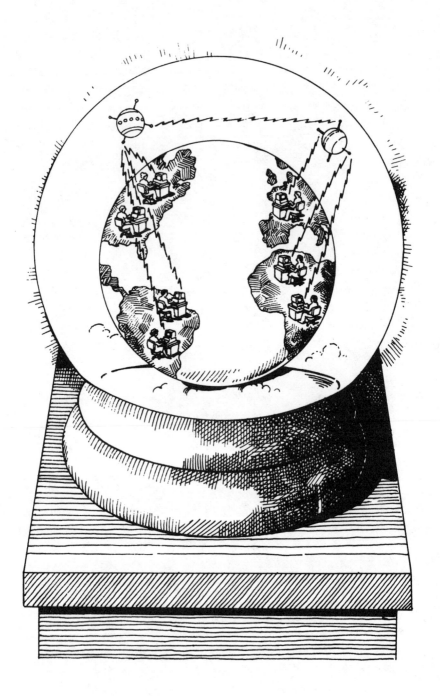

13

What's Next?

The Future of Computer Networking

Gazing into a crystal ball to see the future of electronic networks is both hard and easy. It's easy in the sense that anything you can imagine will probably happen somewhere, sometime. It's hard, on the other hand, because the precise forms that networks will take is difficult to guess. In making predictions for 1984, Doug Clapp, contributing editor of *InfoWorld*, says that microcomputer predictions are easy. "Just predict the same stuff, only bigger, faster and with more doodads." The same is true with networks.

The existing networks will undoubtedly grow bigger, offer more options, and throw in more bells and whistles. New networks are bound to spring up as more and more people have networking capability. It seems to me that the greatest opportunity for innovation and growth lies with the regional networks. The Source, CompuServe and Delphi cover the national information utility scene quite well, and BBSs have been around long enough and are of a type that seems unlikely to change dramatically. Regional networks, however, are just beginning and are searching for their niche.

Bigger and Better

Once a large number of computer owners have communications capability, there is no reason that any location cannot support several specialized regional services. Education, politics, matchmaking and news are just a few of the areas that are ideal for regional coverage. The benefits of regional services are that they can be reasonably priced, can focus on issues of interest to their customer base and can be tailored to fit whatever needs arise.

The existing utilities, databases and services will no doubt grow to meet whatever customer needs arise. Almost all of the utilities are open to suggestion, willing to consider an individual's proposal for a new idea and eager to be everything to everybody. At least for the next few years, new items will be added rapidly to their schedules. Any dramatic changes in local bulletin boards will have to come in the form of software or some way for BBS operators to make money off the deals. As long as they are kind enough to provide free service, what they offer will be fairly straightforward and similar to what exists today. The biggest benefit of letting sysops make a little money would be that they could invest in systems that allow more than one caller on at a time.

Everyone who knows anything about computers keeps saying that it will be five years or more before the software catches up with the hardware. If they are right, and I have no reason to question their judgment, there will probably be all sorts of new communications software developed which will make networking an easier and friendlier process. Software which can be used to access specific databases and utilities is already being offered, and it seems only reasonable to expect more of that kind of thing. The price of software should continue to fall. Software is undoubtedly expensive to develop, but with the growing number of people who want to communicate with computers, software developers can make their profit in volume and make the products accessible to more people.

Talking Keyboards

One interesting possibility for networking is the option of having voice control rather than keyboard control of the computer. Already in the works, this system will allow you to dial up a utility, tell it what you want to do, tell it when you are finished—all without ever having to touch the keyboard. If this path is followed and enough people want it, computer communication will be more like telephone communication. Of course, it is also possible to have the computer talk to you rather than print lines on the screen.

That all sounds a little silly to me, but personal preferences being what they are, it may be the wave of the future. Personally, I'd rather punch on machines than talk to them, and I hate for them to talk to me. "Mike," a friendly computer that dials you up and gives you a sales pitch on the phone, has not been met with open arms by most people I know. Part of the distaste is the sales pitch, but part of it is also the unhuman quality of good old Mike's voice. As the technology stands now and for the foreseeable future, machines just don't sound like real people and the rhythm of their speech is irritating at best.

Speech synthesizing computers and voice-activated computers are godsends for people with handicaps, providing much-needed communications help for them. No doubt, development in these areas will continue. Another group of people who prefer voice-activated machines are those "typophobics" who simply cannot bring themselves to type on anything. Executive types are already accustomed to sitting around in rooms by themselves talking into machines, so the shift from dictaphone to computer will be simple.

Telecommuting

One of the big questions that is already being debated, and that will continue to be debated for years to come, centers around telecommuting. Telecommuting means that you "commute" to your job via the telephone. Theoretically, many people could work at home with home computers and networks connecting them to their offices.

There are several obvious benefits of telecommuting. For the employee, the hassles and cost of traffic, travel, wardrobe, and child care would be minimized. A person could choose where to live without giving any consideration to proximity to the office. For the employer, cost of maintaining office space could be drastically reduced.

Another potential benefit is having more time to spend with family members and neighbors in the home environment. Now this would be a benefit to some but a definite disadvantage to others. Some people, particularly women, go to work precisely because they don't want to stay at home all day. Others find that, however much they love their mates and offspring, twenty-four-hour-a-day togetherness is a bit much. The theory goes something like this: by working at home, parents are allowed more time with each other and their children. A closer nuclear family grows; neighbors become involved with each other and with neighborhood concerns. The old ties that once bound close-knit tribes will once again assert themselves and we will all find satisfaction in the bosom of the group in which we choose to live.

It is a nice theory, and maybe it will work—for some people. I can't help thinking that it depends a great deal on the people and the job. One group that opposes the idea of telecommuting is the Service Employees International Union (SEIU). A union representing 750,000 clerical and health workers, the SEIU maintains that the employee is the one who will get the short end of the telecommuting stick. Because employees will remain somewhat invisible to employers, they will likely get fewer benefits, lower pay and less frequent raises, promotions and advanced training opportunities. Anyone who has ever worked in an office knows that all sorts of subtle things go on before benefits and pay are increased. The old adage about the squeaky wheel getting greased also applies to office facts of life. Generally, to get anything done, someone has to talk and agitate and aggravate until something new is added.

Clerical workers, including data entry clerks, are usually at the bottom of the corporate ladder and are often ignored anyway when upper rungs are opened. If a person is not present to make his or her work known, promotions can be much more difficult to get. Although the benefits of working in an old bathrobe might be worth it to some, they will not be for others. Again it depends on the person.

What kind of work you are doing is also important in how satisfactory telecommuting will be. If your job is to answer the phone for six product managers, you probably won't be able to do it from your ranch. If you're painting the next Mona Lisa, however, you'd probably better stay home and work and take care of your business by electronic mail. Between these extremes, there are a lot of grey areas. Data entry personnel can enter data at home as well as at the office—maybe. If they have quiet time to work, are disciplined in setting aside the time, enjoy being in the midst of their own begonias and hearing Willie Nelson on their own stereo, it could easily lessen stress and make earning money much more pleasant. If, however, they have three kids under four years of age, at least one of whose nose is always running; the Avon lady, struggling magazine salesmen and the guy next door in the middle of his midlife crisis always ringing the doorbell; and a compulsion to wash each dish as it becomes dirty, the stress of working can increase dramatically and what was once an eight-hour day stretches into twelve or fourteen hours.

Aside from earning a necessary living, working at a job provides for other needs we sometimes overlook. Going to work lets you meet people. It often provides an element of surprise in that you can't predict what will happen every day in a busy office. It even gives you an excuse to get dressed and go somewhere—something that some of us need to get us out of bed every morning. Going to work can expand your horizons or it can be stultifying, depending on where you work and what you do.

If your workplace is centered on production, is a place where people don't count and chatting is not allowed, you might greatly benefit from working at home and taking your coffee break to listen to that guy next door. The debate goes on and on and will continue to go on for several years. The fact is that the question cannot finally be decided for everyone in every job. It has to be an individual decision based on your personality, your goals and your needs.

In the final analysis, telecommuting will become what we make it. It has the potential for bringing work down to human scale, enriching the quality of our lives and reducing stressful demands. Regrettably, it also has the potential for further dehumanization, more mindless drudgery and fewer personal rewards. Electronic networking can truly benefit the people who use it only if they keep the human element foremost in their minds.

Tele-Teaching

Work is not the only place where networks can have an influence on our lives. All the chapters in this book describe ways that people are using and can use networks to have more fun, get more done and spend time more productively. Many of those endeavors are just now getting started and the future will see them growing and maturing. Education and politics will undoubtedly become more and more reliant on networks.

Combinations of networks plus personal instruction can benefit both students and instructors by making class attendance easier for the student and making more pedagogical resources available to the teacher. All levels of education will certainly become involved with networking. Because many public schools already have computers, the option of networking can greatly enhance what they will do for the students. Students can talk with other students in broad geographic areas and get firsthand information about the culture and traditions of other areas. They can join in classes originating all over the world. And they can use the facilities of information utilities for any number of projects. It seems quite likely that information-gathering instruction will change quickly as people learn the ease and thoroughness of database search. Just as kids are now taught about the Dewey decimal system and the *Reader's Guide to Periodicals*, they will be taught how to search in Dialog or Orbit or BRS.

The public library catalogue of Colorado Springs is already on-line so that anyone can call up and check to see if a book is available. This limited-function kind of network is bound to become more popular. Networks for public libraries, networks for political information, networks for newspaper subscriptions or electric service, or any other routine procedure are bound to evolve in the future. More libraries, as well as other services, will go on-line.

Colleges and universities will also use networks more often to broaden the selection of courses that students can take. The opportunities to listen to outstanding scholars through networks can make the learning experience more valuable and more exciting. The networks also provide much more computer power than many smaller schools can provide so that students can dial into remote systems to do research of either fact-finding or theoretical nature.

Tele-Campaigning

In politics, networks will surely become more widely used as ways to conduct polls, garner support, spread campaign messages, and perhaps even vote electronically are developed. Many political efforts that founder do so because people do not have the time and energy to knock on doors, make phone calls or stuff envelopes in great enough quantity to get the job done. Electronic networks can do away with much of the tedious work and give people a genuine opportunity to make informed decisions about political matters.

Networks also have great potential in bettering communications between nations. The ongoing discussions about nuclear armament are a sample of the kinds of discussions that could ultimately influence international policies. Networks between the leaders of countries and networks between citizens could do much to lessen the tensions of the world situation.

Talking Back to Talking Pictures

One of the future options of networking that is already being developed is interactive television. As television exists today, they send it out and we take it in. Our only options with regard to programming are to watch a show or turn it off. With interactive television, watchers could participate in the way the program happens. Perhaps your favorite soap opera is depicting the villian embroiled in a passionate embrace with your heroine. Does that just disgust you? Well, tell them! If enough viewers share your opinions, your heroine will give that villian a well-placed chop on his glass jaw. If, however, you figure they deserve each other, you can signal your approval and the plot will continue. Such possibilities are just around the corner.

Probably the ability to communicate with television stations, networks and specific programs will not be universal, but the option will undoubtedly exist. The Neilsen ratings will become obsolete as networkers direct comments to the people who make decisions about what we see on TV. You may even be able to question witnesses on "People's Court" or grill guests on the Donahue show or match wits with celebrities on "Hollywood Squares."

Questions to be Answered

There are a few problems to be faced and questions to be answered as electronic networking develops. One of the questions centers on the gaps in society that are developing as a result of the information age. Are people who are not computer literate going to become a disadvantaged class? Are women and other minorities—who do not have access or do not want access to computers—going to find themselves left out? Is a socioeconomic gap going to grow out of this information revolution which will create new and greater problems? If networking is to reach its potential as a uniting and freeing force in education, politics and other areas of life, some provisions must be made which will include all sections of the population.

Creative, nontechnical people must be drawn into networking so that new ideas can develop. It is my guess that the great technical breakthroughs of the next ten years will come from nontechnical people who have fewer preconceptions about what computers can do. The technical folks will, perhaps, have to implement the ideas, but innovation itself may come from another source.

Electronic networking will never take the place of a warm hand or a comforting hug. The clicking of keys cannot soothe like the sound of a beloved voice. Total communication through networks is neither likely nor desirable. Networks provide a special kind of communication. They can put you in touch with many people you could not otherwise reach. But the communication is very much on a mental level. Somehow, someone has got to devise a way to touch the emotions and spirit of people before the networks can be a full-service way for people to communicate.

14

I'll Byte (or What Does That Mean Again?)

Glossary of Computerese

This glossary of computer jargon is not meant to be complete or comprehensive. Words that you are most likely to run into as you network are included with brief, nontechnical explanations. If you want more technical or more detailed information, consult a dictionary. Several dictionaries of computer terms are available.

ACCESS—to get into a system and store or retrieve data from it.

ACOUSTIC COUPLER—a device that connects your computer to other computers through phone lines. A type of modem in which your phone receiver fits into cups that are attached to the modem.

APPLICATION—a particular use for electronic systems. Word processing, payroll and accounting are applications.

ASCII—(pronounced ass' kee) acronym for American Standard Code for Information Interchange—the standard code for transmitting data from one place to another.

BASIC—acronym for Beginner's All-purpose Symbolic Instruction Code—a programming language that is easy to learn and is widely used as the first programming language taught. Many children in school are learning BASIC. It is also a common language in microcomputers.

BAUD—a unit of measurement that describes how fast information can be transmitted from one place to another. 300 baud is approximately the transmission of 300 bits per second. The word comes from J. M. E. Baudot, a French pioneer in printing telegraphy.

BINARY—refers to a system in which there are only two numbers—0 and 1. Every number or character is made up of a combination of 0s and 1s. This system resulted from electronic impulses being either off or on, so that there are only two signals which are combined in different ways to symbolize different characters or numbers.

BIT—a contraction of Binary DigIT—the smallest unit of storage in the computer. Each character is made up of 8 bits. A bit is either a 0 or a 1.

BOOT—To start up your machine. When you turn the computer on, put in your diskette and get it going, you are "booting up" the machine. There are "warm boots" and "cold boots," not as any normal person would expect for winter and summer, but to make the machine load either part or all of the program into its memory.

BPS—Bits Per Second—the same as BAUD—the rate at which data is transferred from one place to another.

BUFFER—an area for storing data temporarily when it is being transferred from one device to another.

BYTE—a group of bits which together form a unit, such as a letter or number. Usually bytes contain eight bits.

CABLE—a bundle of insulated wires which electronic currents pass through. Cables connect computers to printers and modems to send signals back and forth.

CARRIAGE RETURN—a term left over from typewriter days when the carriage actually returned. On computers the key is called "carriage return," "return" or "enter," and generally indicates to the computer that you are finished with that piece of information and are ready to move on to something else.

CARRIER—a signal provided by telephone or telegraph lines that connects you with a remote device through communication lines. When you are connected, you have a carrier. If your machine says "No Carrier," that means you have no line of communication. Hang up the phone.

CPU—Central Processing Unit—the part of your computer that does the work.

CHARACTER—any of the symbols on the keys on your keyboard. A character can be a letter, number, punctuation mark or special symbol.

CHIP—1. an electronic circuit created on a tiny silicon flake upon which many gates and paths are connected. The chip can be used for memory or processing. The chip consumes little power and is compact and inexpensive. It is the key to computers, digital watches, and the electronic age. 2. The name of many people in the technical department.

COMMAND—what you tell the computer to do. For example, a Print command would set in motion whatever electronics are necessary to print your file.

COMPUTERESE—all this stuff. The specialized language that has developed around computer science.

CONNECT TIME—the amount of time that your computer is connected to another computer, measured from the time you sign on until you sign off.

CONTROL KEY—the key on your computer which is marked "CONTROL" or "CTRL" which, used in conjunction with other keys, makes them do special things. "CONTROL S," for example, usually stops temporarily whatever is happening on your screen. If you are told to enter "Control K," you hold down the control key while typing the letter key.

CP/M—abbreviation for Control Program for Microprocessors. A popular operating system widely used on microcomputers developed by Digital Research, Inc.

CRASH—an emergency. When your system becomes inoperable for one reason or another and what you have done disappears forever. Crashes can be caused by system malfunctions or by the operator.

CRT—an abbreviation for Cathode Ray Tube. A screen like a television screen that is used with computers for viewing what is going on. CRTs vary in size and color.

CURSOR—a visual indicator of where you are on the screen. The cursor can be a flashing light, a block of light or a line under your current character. It moves along with you as you work.

DAISY WHEEL PRINTER—a letter-quality printer that prints one letter at a time by moving a little wheel to position the correct letter for printing. Each letter is individually printed by the wheel impacting against a printing ribbon.

DATA—characters grouped together in specific patterns to which meaning is assigned. Any words, numbers, characters or symbols put into or taken out of a computer are data.

DATABASE—a grouping of data arranged so that pieces of the data can be extracted from the whole.

DEBUG—the process of finding out what is wrong with hardware or software and fixing it.

DEFAULT—what the computer does unless you tell it to do something else. The default speed of your computer may be 1200 baud and this may be changed by telling it to slow down to 300 baud.

DISK—a piece of hardware on which software is commonly stored. Data are stored magnetically on disks in concentric circular paths called tracks.

DISK DRIVE—a unit that reads and writes data stored on disks.

DISKETTE—a floppy disk, the most commonly used disks for microcomputers. Diskettes come in 5 1/4 and 8 inch sizes.

DOCUMENTATION—the material that tells you how to operate your hardware and/or your software. Good documentation should include both technical and nontechnical information about the product described.

DOT MATRIX—characters or printers that create symbols by groups of tiny dots rather than by creating them all at once as a typewriter does.

DOWN—indicates the state of a not-working computer. What the computer always is when you call about a mistake in your bill.

DOWNLOAD—the ability to save material from an on-line session by storing it on a diskette or printing it on a printer. Downloading refers to data coming "down" the phone line to your computer.

DUMB TERMINAL—a piece of hardware that allows you to send and receive data, but does not allow you to do anything else. It has no memory, does not process data, does not compute. It must be connected to a computer to do anything.

EDIT—to change, add or delete data in a file.

ELECTRONIC MAIL—messages sent from one person to another by electronic means.

ENTER KEY—same as Carriage Return key.

EXPANDABLE— indicates that a computer can be made to do

additional things by adding more devices to it. A computer is expandable if it allows you to connect a printer, add extra memory, add more disk drives.

FATAL ERROR—dramatics in the computer world. This is an error in a program which stops the program in progress and probably loses whatever you were doing.

FILE—a collection of data that is related. You create a file when you start something new on your computer. You end the file when you are ready to do something else. You open and close files that you have already created. File is also used as a verb: you file something when you are finished working on it.

FIRMWARE—a program built into your hardware which you can use but not change.

FLOPPY—an abbreviation of Floppy Disk.

FLOPPY DISK—a disk made of mylar which can be magnetized to store data. Usually 5 1/4 or 8 inches in diameter, the disk is flexible, hence its name. The same as a diskette.

FORMAT—the defined arrangement of data. Computers require different formats, so disks must be formatted to use on your particular machine, and software is not interchangeable because of differences in formatting.

FULL DUPLEX—indicates that data are being transmitted in two directions at the same time. You are sending data at the same time that the person you are communicating with is sending data.

FUNCTION KEY—a key on your computer that is dedicated to one operation. The "return" key is a function key because it does one thing. Some computers allow keys to be programmed as function keys.

HALF DUPLEX—indicates that data are being sent in only one direction at a time. You send your data, then the other person sends data.

HARD COPY—computer-generated information that is printed on paper.

HARDWARE—the physical equipment of a computer system.

ILLEGAL CHARACTER—more drama. This means that the computer can't recognize and understand the character you've typed in the context in which you've typed it.

ILLEGAL OPERATION—instructions that the computer can't follow.

INFORMATION—data that have been processed by a human. Information results when data are given meaning and significance.

INPUT—the things you type into the computer.

INTERACTIVE—back and forth. An interactive program is one that works with you and allows changes without requiring re-programming.

I/O—abbreviation for Input/Output.

JOY STICK—a manual control device connected to a computer for manipulation of the cursor. It is commonly used in computer graphics and game playing.

LINE FEED—movement of a printing mechanism to the next line. Printers and printing terminals use line feed to keep the machine from printing one line on top of the last.

LOAD—to transfer data from storage to the memory of the computer. You load a program into the machine when you put in your disk and start it running.

LOG—to connect something to something else. You log one disk drive to another or one system to another.

LOG IN—to enter whatever information is necessary to connect you to another system.

LOG OFF—to enter whatever information is necessary to disconnect you from another system.

LOG ON—same as Log In.

LOG OUT—same as Log Off.

MACHINE ERROR—something that can't be blamed on you. An error in the program caused by a malfunction of the computer or its related equipment.

MAINFRAME—a large central processing unit and the equipment that contains that unit.

MEGABIT—one million bits.

MEGABYTE—one million bytes.

MEMORY—a device that can store data and allows data to be retrieved from it.

MENU—a display listing the choices of things you can do on the particular system you are using.

MICRO—a shortened form of "microcomputer."

MICROCOMPUTER—a small, relatively inexpensive computer which contains a microprocessor. It contains random access memory, read-only memory and is useful for a wide variety of purposes.

198

MICROPROCESSOR—the chip that contains the electronic directions to make your microcomputer work.

MINICOMPUTER— a midsized computer that can support several users and large amounts of data.

MODE—the condition or method of operation. Chat mode, for example, is a situation in which you can talk back and forth with another person.

MODEM—acronym for MOdulator-DEModulator. A device that allows you to connect your computer to other computers through telephone lines.

MONITOR—the screen of your CRT.

MOUSE—a hand-held device that moves over a pad and controls the cursor on your CRT. Commonly used in computer graphics to plot points on a graph.

NULL—emptiness, no characters. Nulls are used to provide space and time for your computer to do what it needs to do.

OFF-LINE—when your computer is working alone and not connected to any other system.

ON-LINE—when your computer is connected to another system.

OPERATING SYSTEM—a collection of programs that controls the overall operation of your computer. Operating systems in microcomputers differ, therefore software must differ.

OUTPUT—data that result from computer operations—either hard copy or on the screen.

PACKET SWITCHING—a method of sending data from one point to another in groups of bits. Each packet is sent separately. Telenet and Tymnet are packet-switching systems that transfer your data to another system and send theirs to you.

PARALLEL TRANSMISSION—when data are sent from your computer to somewhere else one character at a time. Eight bits travel side by side from your computer to the receiver. Transmission to the printer is usually parallel. Transmission through phone lines is not.

PASSWORD—a group of characters by which you are identified by a system not your own. Your password is unique to you and allows the system you are using to recognize you.

PERIPHERAL—any add-on equipment for your central processing unit.

POWER DOWN—to turn it off.

POWER UP—to turn it on.

PROGRAM—a set of instructions that tell the computer what to do.

PROGRAMMABLE FUNCTION KEYS—keys that can be made to issue a series of commands with a single key stroke. Keys can be programmed to dial CompuServe, type in your User ID and Password—all with one stroke of the key.

PROMPT—the character a system uses to tell you it's your turn to do something. Prompts can be "!" or ":" or "*" or anything else the programmer decides. When you see a prompt, it is the signal for you to issue a command.

RAM—acronym for Random Access Memory. The memory in your computer that can be accessed directly. That part of memory which is used to store what you are working on until you save it on a disk. Your programs are also put into RAM when you are using them.

REAL TIME—communications that take place in real time are those that allow people to communicate directly with each other through their computers. There is no message leaving, delay for transmission, or such. Chat mode is real time as are several other options.

REMOTE—devices that are separated by space but can still work together through communications links.

REMOTE ACCESS—the ability to send and receive data through communications lines to distant computers.

RETURN KEY—see Carriage Return.

ROM—acronym for Read-Only Memory. The part of your computer's memory that you cannot change. Part of the operating system is stored here.

ROS—abbreviation for Read-Only Storage. The material in your ROM can be read but not altered.

SCAN—to examine briefly, and in order, items listed. Scan is often a bulletin board option which allows you to decide which entries are interesting enough to read.

SCROLL—the movement of data up and down your screen. You can scroll continuously until you are ready to stop and read or do something with the information you see.

SERIAL TRANSMISSION—the sending of one bit of information after another in a line. Transmissions on phone lines must be serial and require a serial port or card to translate your data into that form.

SIGN OFF—same as "Log Off."

SIGN ON—same as "Log On."

SOFT COPY—information displayed on your video screen, but not printed on paper.

SOFTWARE—programs, languages and directions that tell computers what to do and how to do it. Software comes packaged on disks, cassettes and cartridges. Or you can write your own.

SPECIAL SYMBOL (OR CHARACTER)—a character that is not a number or letter. "$", "&", "!" are special characters.

SYSTEM—a combination of hardware, software and people working together to get something done.

TELECOMMUNICATION—transmission of data from one point to another by communication lines.

TELECOMMUTING—the ability to work at home on a computer rather than travelling to an office to do the work. Usually the work is sent to the office via a network.

TELETEXT—the system that allows a person to retrieve data on a home television set, but does not allow that person to input data.

TERMINAL—a device for sending and receiving data. Generally composed of a keyboard and either a printer or a monitor.

TEXT—groups of words. This is text as opposed to numerical formulas or programming languages.

TOGGLE—similar to an off-on switch. You can toggle commands by punching a single key to turn a function on and punching that key again to turn it off.

USER—a person who uses a computer system.

USER-FRIENDLY—a describer of hardware, software and other devices indicating that they are easy to use for nontechnical people.

UTILITY—shortened form of Information Utility.

VIDEOTEX OR *VIDEOTEXT*—interactive data-retrieval and communication system that connects a large computer center with a home computer user through telephone lines. Both user and computer can input data.

WORD PROCESSOR—an automated, computerized system used to prepare, edit, store and transmit text.

WRITE—to store data from your computer's memory on a disk.

15

What's That Number?

Resources for the Electronic Networker

DATABASES AND SERVICES

BRS
Bibliographic Retrieval Services
1200 Rte. 7
Latham, NY 12110
(800) 833-4707

BRS/AFTER DARK
Bibliographic Retrieval Services
1200 Rte. 7
Latham, NY 12110
(800) 833-4707

C.A.R.O.L.
Computer Assisted Research
On Line
Bob Sherman
1166 N.E. 182 St.
North Miami Beach, FL 33160
(305) 944-2111

CHASE ECONOMETRICS
Chase Econometrics/Interactive
Data Corporation
486 Totten Pond Rd.
Waltham, MA 02154
(617) 890-1234

CITISHARE CORPORATION
850 3rd Ave.
New York, NY 10043
(212) 572-9605

COLLECTOR'S DATA SERVICE
420 West Mercer
Seattle, WA 98119
(800) 435-0100
(206) 281-7273 in Washington

COMPUSERVE
Consumer Information Service
5000 Arlington Center Blvd.
P. O. Box 20212
Columbus, OH 43220
(800) 848-8199
in Ohio
(614) 457-0802

DELPHI
General Videotex Corporation
3 Blackstone St.
Cambridge, MA 02139
(617) 491-3393

DIALOG
Dialog Information Services, Inc.
3460 Hillview Ave.
Palo Alto, CA 94304
(800) 227-1927
(800) 982-5838
DOW JONES NEWS/RETRIEVAL
Dow Jones and Company, Inc.
P. O. Box 300
Princeton, NJ 08540
(800) 257-5114
(609) 452-1511 in New Jersey
E-COM
United States Postal Service
call your local Post Office
EDNET
National Education Corporation
315 Post Rd.
Westport, CT 06880
(203) 227-0891
EIES
Electronic Information Exchange System
Computerized Conferencing and Communications Center
323 High St.
Newark, NJ 07102
(201) 645-5221
ELECTRONIC UNIVERSITY
TeleLearning Systems, Inc.
505 Beach St.
San Francisco, CA 94133
(415) 928-2800
THE ELECTRIC PAGES
P. O. Box 2550
Austin, TX 78768
(512) 472-6432

THE ELECTRONIC EDITION
Official Airlines Guides, Inc.
2000 Clearwater Dr.
Oak Brook, IL 60521
(312) 654-6000
HAM RADIO NETWORK
Chesapeake Microcomputer Club
Joe Kasser, President
11532 Stewart Ln.
Silver Spring, MD 20904
ITT DIALCOM
ITT Dialcom, Inc.
1109 Spring St.
Silver Spring, MD 20910
(301) 588-1572
THE INFORMATION BANK
New York Times Information Service
1719A—Route 10
Parsippany, NJ 07054
(201) 539-5850
(212) 683-2208 in New York
(793) 243-7220 in Washington, D.C.
(312) 236-6800 in Chicago
(415) 522-2600 in San Francisco
(213) 852-7003 in Los Angeles
(713) 965-9371 in Houston
(416) 598-5250 in Toronto
KNOWLEDGE INDEX
Dialog Information Services, Inc.
3460 Hillview Ave.
Palo Alto, CA 94304
(800) 227-5510
(415) 858-3796 in California
(800) 227-1927 (Dialog)

MCI MAIL
(800) 323-7751 to register by
computer
(800) MCI-2255 for information

NEWSNET
945 Haverford Rd.
Bryn Mawr, PA 19010
(800) 345-1301
(215) 527-8030

NITE-LINE
National Computer Network
1929 Harlem Ave.
Chicago, IL 60635
(312) 622-6666

ORBIT
SDC Information Services
2500 Colorado Ave.
Santa Monica, CA 90406
(800) 421-7229
(800) 352-6689 in California

PARTICIPATE
Participation Systems, Inc.
43 Myrtle Ter.
Winchester, MA 01890
(617) 729-1976

PLATO
Control Data Corporation
Call the CDC office nearest
you, or
Minneapolis, MN
(800) 328-1109

SEARCHMART
Searchmart Corporation
636 U. S. Highway 1, Suite 210
North Palm Beach, FL 33408
(305) 845-2996

THE SOURCE
Source Telecomputing
Corporation
1616 Anderson Rd.
McLean, VA 22102
(800) 336-3366
(703) 734-7540 in Virginia

TELENET
GTE Telenet
8229 Boone Blvd.
Vienna, VA 22180
(703) 827-9565
(800) 336-0437
(800) 572-0408 in Virginia

TYMNET
Tymshare, Inc.
20705 Valley Green Dr.
Cupertino, CA 95014
(408) 446-6236
(800) 336-0149 in the East
(800) 323-7389 in the West

**WESTERN UNION
EASYLINK**
(800) 336-3797 ext. 108
(703) 448-8877 ext. 108 in
Virginia

DIRECTORIES AND PUBLICATIONS

COMPUTER-READABLE
DATABASES
American Society for
Information Science
1010 16th St. NW
Washington, D.C. 20036
(202) 659-3644

COMPUTER-READABLE
DATABASES:
A DIRECTORY AND DATA
SOURCEBOOK
Knowledge Industry
Publications, Inc.
701 Winchester Ave.
White Plains, NY 10604
(914) 328-9157

DATACAST
Wireless Digital, Inc.
345 Sweet Rd.
Woodside, CA 94062
(415) 851-2814

DATAPRO DIRECTORY OF
ON-LINE SERVICES
Datapro Research Corporation
1805 Underwood Blvd.
Delran, NJ 08075
(609) 764-0100

DIRECTORY OF FEDERAL
STATISTICAL DATA FILES
National Technical Information
Service
5285 Port Royal Rd.
Springfield, VA 22161
(804) 487-4600

DIRECTORY OF ONLINE
DATABASES
Cuadra Associates, Inc.
2001 Wilshire Blvd., Suite 305
Santa Monica, CA 90403
(213) 829-9972

ELECTRONIC MAIL &
MESSAGE SYSTEMS (EMMS)
International Resource
Development
30 High St.
Norwalk, CT 06851
(203) 866-6914

ENCYCLOPEDIA OF
INFORMATION SYSTEMS
AND SERVICES
Gale Research Company
Book Tower
Detroit, MI 48226
(313) 961-2242

INFORMATION INDUSTRY
MARKETPLACE
R.R. Bowker and Company
1180 Sixth Ave.
New York, NY 10036
(212) 764-5100

INFORMATION SOURCES
Information Industry
Association
316 Pennsylvania Ave, SE
Suite 400
Washington, DC 20003
(202) 544-1969

MICROCOMPUTER
INFORMATION SUPPORT
TOOLS (MIST)
Peter and Trudy Johnson-Lenz
695 Fifth St.
Lake Oswego, OR 97034
(503) 635-2615

ONLINE and DATABASE
Online, Inc.
11 Tannery Ln.
Weston, CT 06883
(203) 227-8466
**THE ON-LINE COMPUTER
TELEPHONE DIRECTORY**
J. A. Cambron Company, Inc.
P. O. Box 10005
Kansas City, MO 64111
(816) 756-1847
CompuServe 70040,414
OTHER NETWORKS
P. O. Box 14066
Philadelphia, PA 19123

**SPACE RESEARCH
NEWSLETTER**
Steven K. Moyer
P. O. Box 803
State College, PA 16801
(814) 238-2279
Delphi: SPACEMAN
VIDEOPRINT
International Resource
Development
30 High St.
Norwalk, CT 06851
(203) 866-6914

BOOKS

*The Complete Handbook of
Personal Computer
Communications*
by Alfred Glossbrenner
St. Martin's Press
New York, NY
1983
The Computer Phone Book
by Mike Cane
New American Library, 1983
(Updates available from:
Mike Cane
The Computer Phone Book
175 Fifth Ave., Suite 3371
New York, NY 10010)
Hooking In
by Tom Beeston & Tom Tucker
ComputerFood Press
Westlake Village, CA
1983

*How to Create Your Own
Computer Bulletin Board*
by Lary L. Myers
TAB Books, Inc.
Blue Ridge Summit, PA
1983
*The Network Nation: Human
Communication via Computer*
by Murray Turoff and Starr
Roxanne Hiltz
Addison-Wesley
Reading, MA
1978
*The Network Revolution:
Confessions of a Computer
Scientist*
by Jacques Vallee
And/Or Press, Inc.
Berkeley, CA
1982

The Omni Future Almanac
edited by Robert Weil
Omni Press
World Almanac Publications
New York, NY
1983

Omni Online Database
Directory
by Mike Edelhart and
Owen Davies
Collier Books
Macmillan Publishing
Company
New York, NY
1983

BULLETIN BOARDS

This does not pretend to be a complete listing of BBSs, but it does try to list a variety of types of boards and boards in most areas of the country. It should be enough to get you started. The words in parentheses indicate the features or special area of interest of the board.

ABACUS-BY-PHONE
(General interest, fee charged)
Anchorage, AK
(907) 278-4223

JOE'S COMPUTER
(General)
Montgomery, AL
(205) 288-1100

ARIZONA BULLETIN
BOARD
(Items for sale, general)
Phoenix, AZ
(602) 957-4428

ARK-NET
(General, part-time)
Little Rock, AR
(501) 372-0576

ORACLE BBS
(Gay sex)
Hollywood, CA
(213) 980-5643

INTERACT
(General, issues & discussion)
Sylmar, CA
(213) 367-0324

MINES OF MORIA
(Games)
Aptos, CA
(408) 688-9629

CONFERENCE TREE
(Conferencing)
Berkeley, CA
(408) 475-7101

PMS-GAMEBOARD
(Role-playing games)
San Diego, CA
(619) 283-3574

PMS #1
(General, BBS list, discussion)
Santee, CA
(619) 561-7277

GREENE MACHINE
(General, BBS list,
conferencing)
Napa, CA
(707) 257-1101

*PMS-*IF*MAGAZINE*
(General, home video)
Anaheim, CA
(714) 772-8868

208

BULLET-80
(Public domain software, games)
Sacramento, CA
(916) 971-1395

**OLD COLORADO CITY
ELECTRONIC COTTAGE**
(Writing, politics, general)
Colorado Springs, CO
(303) 632-3391

UFONET
(Parapsychology, UFOs, other)
Golden, CO
(303) 278-4244

EDUCATION-80
(Computers in schools)
Greenwich, CT
(203) 629-4375

FORUM-80
(General)
Wilmington, DE
(302) 762-3170

ARMUDIC
(General)
Washington, D.C.
(202) 276-8342

ALPHA
(Writing, movies, polling)
Tampa, FL
(813) 969-0512

THE NOTEBOOK
(Writing)
West Palm Beach, FL
(305) 686-4862

DR. D'S COCO CORNER
(Color Computer)
Pensacola, FL
(904) 456-7195

**ATLANTA COMPUTER
SOCIETY**
(General, computers)
Atlanta, GA
(404) 636-6130

TRADE-80 MINI BBS
(General)
Albany, GA
(912) 439-7440

CONFERENCE TREE
(Conferencing)
Honolulu, HI
(808) 487-2001

WORD EXCHANGE
(General)
Springfield, IL
(217) 753-4309

JAMS
(General, public domain
software)
Lockport, IL
(815) 838-1020

**AVC—COMMODORE
BULLETIN BOARD**
(Commodore computers)
Indianapolis, IN
(317) 255-5435

**APPLE MEDICAL
BULLETIN BOARD**
(Medicine, part-time)
Iowa City, IA
(319) 353-6528

**DICKENSON'S MOVIE
GUIDE**
(Movie reviews)
Mission, KN
(913) 432-5544

TBBS
(General)
Shreveport, LA
(318) 635-8660

RCP/M
(Atari computers, CP/M)
Baton Rouge, LA
(504) 273 3116

**PROGRAMMER'S
ANONYMOUS**
(Osborne computers, general)
Gorham, ME
(207) 839-2337
GASNET
(Space program)
Beltsville, MD
(301) 344-9156
TBBS
(General)
Springfield, MA
(413) 733-1749
**LAWRENCE GENERAL
HOSPITAL**
(Medical)
Boston, MA
(617) 683-2119
BARTON DATA LINE
(General, BBS list)
Ann Arbor, MI
(313) 662-8303
COMPUNET
(General)
Lansing, MI
(517) 339-3367
GRASS
(Atari computers)
Grand Rapids, MI
(616) 241-1971
THE JOB SYSTEM
(Computer-related
employment)
Minneapolis, MN
(612) 542-9597
LAWSIG
(Computer-related law)
Minneapolis, MN
(612) 872-2352
CBBS
(Christensen & Suess)
Kansas City, MO
(312) 546-8086

HAM BBS
(Ham radio, games)
Independence, MO
(816) 833-3427
SOUTHERN BULLET
(General)
Hattiesburg, MS
(601) 264-2361
ABBS
(General, CP/M)
Omaha, NE
(402) 292-9598
MAGAZINE-80
(Writing, TRS computers)
Peterborough, NH
(603) 924-7920
LIMERICKS
(Limericks, trivia)
New Brunswick, NJ
(201) 572-0617
ED GELB'S DATA BASE
(Real Estate, BBS lists)
Wayne, NJ
(201) 694-7425
PHOTO-80
(Photography)
Haledon, NJ
(201) 790-6795
PMS-CENTURY 23
(General)
Las Vegas, NV
(702) 878-9106
BULL—PC
(IBM PC)
New York, NY
(212) 490-1146
**PMS—MCGRAW-HILL BOOK
COMPANY**
(Mail, book catalogue shopping)
New York, NY
(212) 512-2488

TICKERSCREEN
(Stock market)
New York, NY
(212) 986-1660

LICA
(General, computer)
Bethpage, NY
(516) 561-6590

PC-BBS
(General, computers)
Charlotte, NC
(704) 365-4311

PMS-RAUG
(General)
Akron, OH
(216) 867-7463

INDEPENDENT BBS
(General)
Toledo, OH
(419) 729-4221

TBBS
(General, adult)
Tulsa, OK
(918) 749-0059

BIT BUCKET BBS
(General)
Portland, OR
(503) 761-6345

RCP/M
(Atari computers)
Cheltenham, PA
(215) 836-5116

FORUM-80
(General, BBS list)
Memphis, TN
(901) 276 8196

TBBS
(General)
Austin, TX
(512) 385-1102

THE AUSTIN PARTY BOARD
(General, adult)
Austin, TX
(512) 442-1116

THE ARMADILLO
(General, Atari computers)
Austin, TX
(512) 837-2003

THE TEXAS LEPRECHAUN
(General)
Austin, TX
(512) 288-2114

TBBS #1
(General, computers)
Austin, TX
(512) 385-1102

THE DINER
(General interest)
Austin, TX
(512) 443-3084

TEXAS T-NET
(General)
Austin, TX
(512) 345-8290

BURG BOARD
(General, fiction games)
Amarillo, TX
(806) 374-9711

TBBS
(General, computer)
San Angelo, TX
(915) 942-8035

TBBS
(TRS computers, Orch-90)
Tyler, TX
(214) 566-1374

COMMODORE CENTRAL
(Commodore computers, BBS
list)
Holladay, UT
(801) 277-3913

CBBS AMRAD
(Ham radio, broad range of
technical information)
McLean, VA
(703) 734-1387
DIAL-YOUR-MATCH #32
(Matchmaking)
Newport News, VA
(804) 838-3973
MAILBOARD 82.1
(General, BBS list)
Seattle, WA
(206) 527-0897

TBBS
(General, BBS list)
Comet, WV
(304) 273-4136
CANOPUS
(General, teenagers)
Greenfield, WI
(414) 281-0545
COMMODORE BULLETIN BOARD
(Commodore computers, BBS list)
Cheyenne, WY
(307) 637-6045

Index

Acknowledgments

Few books are completed by an author alone. Many people were involved in making this book a reality:

Special thanks must go to Ray Bard for his ideas, patience, support and counsel. The book would have never been done without his efforts.

Charles Horni provided essential and "user friendly" technical advice in addition to making my computer work so I could do the fun part.

Larry Wolfe came to the rescue at the last minute with additional technical expertise.

Mary Ann Noretto contributed her skill and talent in design and and typography.

Mike Krone provided the delightful illustrations.

Jeff Morris helped it all make sense through his excellent and often entertaining editing.

Execucom allowed me the flexibility in my job to be able to spend the time required to research and write the book.

Although individual credit can't be given here, the many networkers who shared their stories, put together entertaining, informative and eye-opening systems and offered technical advice are the backbone and inspiration for this book.

Finally, and very importantly, Sarah and Jenny Spurgin, my daughters, cheerfully put up with it all.

Without the help of all these people, I could have never finished this book, and to them goes my sincere gratitude.